JOSSEY-BASS TEACHER

Jossey-Bass Teacher provides K–12 teachers with essential knowledge and tools to create a positive and lifelong impact on student learning. Trusted and experienced educational mentors offer practical classroom-tested and theory-based teaching resources for improving teaching practice in a broad range of grade levels and subject areas. From one educator to another, we want to be your first source to make every day your best day in teaching. *Jossey-Bass Teacher* resources serve two types of informational needs—essential knowledge and essential tools.

Essential knowledge resources provide the foundation, strategies, and methods from which teachers may design curriculum and instruction to challenge and excite their students. Connecting theory to practice, essential knowledge books rely on a solid research base and time-tested methods, offering the best ideas and guidance from many of the most experienced and well-respected experts in the field.

Essential tools save teachers time and effort by offering proven, ready-to-use materials for in-class use. Our publications include activities, assessments, exercises, instruments, games, ready reference, and more. They enhance an entire course of study, a weekly lesson, or a daily plan. These essential tools provide insightful, practical, and comprehensive materials on topics that matter most to K–12 teachers.

Prompted to Write

Prompted to Write

BUILDING ON-DEMAND

WRITING SKILLS, GRADES 6–12

Meredith Pike-Baky

Gerald Fleming

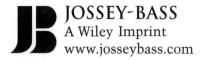
JOSSEY-BASS
A Wiley Imprint
www.josseybass.com

Published by Jossey-Bass
A Wiley Imprint
989 Market Street, San Francisco, CA 94103-1741   www.josseybass.com

Jossey-Bass books and products are available through most bookstores. To contact Jossey-Bass directly call our Customer Care Department within the U.S. at 800-956-7739, outside the U.S. at 317-572-3986, or fax 317-572-4002.

Jossey-Bass also publishes its books in a variety of electronic formats. Some content that appears in print may not be available in electronic books.

Library of Congress Cataloging-in-Publication Data
Pike-Baky, Meredith, 1948-
   Prompted to write: building on-demand writing skills, grades 6–12 / Meredith Pike-Baky, Gerald Fleming.—1st ed.
     p. cm.—(Jossey-Bass teacher)
  Includes bibliographical references and index.
  ISBN 13 978–0–7879–7457–2
  ISBN 10 0–7879–7457–9 (alk. paper)
  1. Language arts (Secondary) 2. English language—Composition and exercises—Study and teaching (Secondary)
   I. Fleming, Gerald J., 1946- II. Title. III. Series.
LB1631.P55 2005
808'.042'0712—dc22

                  2005013833

Printed in the United States of America
FIRST EDITION
PB Printing   10 9 8 7 6 5 4 3 2 1

CONTENTS

Writing to Inform and Explain

PREFACE

Prompted to Write is a collection of carefully crafted writing lessons, each leading to an assessment, for students in middle and high school, and beyond. Each lesson, an integrated assessment, is designed to deepen literacy and prepare students for on-demand writing tests. Students encounter many of these throughout their academic careers: middle school proficiency tests, high school exit exams, the recently introduced SAT essay, and college placement tests are some examples. This collection of integrated lessons guides students as they improve their ability to write on demand in response to a range of issues for a variety of purposes. The intention is to deepen the dynamics of on-demand writing.

Included herein are fifteen comprehensive, custom-designed performance assessments. Each is an integrated, carefully scaffolded lesson that includes reading, discussion, and planning activities to prepare students before they write. Students move through each stage of the writing process and become adept at writing a complete essay in a limited amount of time. Essay topics are current and compelling and help writers develop versatility by addressing both narrative and expository genres. Step-by-step teacher guidelines for implementing the lessons and suggestions for modifying the assessments are included. A customized holistic rubric is included for each assessment and eleven scored and annotated student examples (two in Chapter Five and the others in Appendix A) guide the teacher (and students) in evaluating the writing.

The book is designed primarily for classroom use; it can form the backbone of a comprehensive year-long writing program or serve as a resource for supplemental units of instruction. The lessons can also be used for larger-scale grade-level or even schoolwide assessments, bringing teachers together across grades and subject areas to focus on student writing. Administering the assessments at key points during the school year gives students, teachers, and parents concrete information about writing development.

We have field-tested these lessons in single classrooms and in multi-district communities. The effort is a natural outgrowth of our work—which began in 1988—to design compelling prompts and refine scoring procedures based on observations of students' steady writing improvement and teachers' keen evaluations. The scaffolded activities in each lesson provide a variety of approaches to developing and organizing ideas; the teacher support and comprehensive scoring guidelines truly do prompt students to write more fluently and skillfully in a limited amount of time.

To respond to the challenges of teaching writing today, a writing program must connect the external demands of test-readiness—conspicuously including the ability to write spontaneously despite time pressure—and the thoughtful process of gracious composition and keen revision. *Prompted to Write* sets out to champion student-centered writing in a test-centered time.

HOW *PROMPTED TO WRITE* WAS DEVELOPED

We've always been intrigued by the power and (sometimes) capriciousness of assessment in students' and teachers' lives. We came to understand the positive power of a quality assessment with CLAS, the integrated reading-writing assessment administered in California in the late 1980s. A holistically scored writing assessment at fourth, eighth, and tenth grades, its teacher-developed prompts integrated reading and group work and provided copious training materials to link instruction to assessment. Though the design proved too expensive to sustain, it taught many of us that process could be efficiently and meaningfully woven into assessment and that holistic evaluation of writing can both recognize what individual student writers do best and reflect real-world writing.

Now, many years later, we continue our work to improve student achievement by way of quality curriculum and assessment. We've witnessed firsthand the power of carefully designed and well-organized assessments as they improve student writing, broaden teachers' repertoire, and increase faculty unity. Each of these outcomes stems from quality writing prompts.

We've gathered a collection of excellent prompts, have developed guidelines for assisting you in using them, and have included a set of annotated student examples to anchor teachers and students in applying the rubrics.

The prompts themselves have been winnowed over many years from among hundreds we've administered in our classrooms, schools, and districts. We've only included prompts proven to work, and by *work* we mean they satisfy these criteria:

- Students respond well and enthusiastically to them.

- The resulting essays are engaging to read.

- Scoring can be done easily and clearly both as an in-class activity and a schoolwide activity.

WAYS TO USE THE BOOK

Prompted to Write is intended to be used at a variety of levels, and they're not mutually exclusive. First, it's designed for classroom-based instruction and assessment. Let's say a classroom teacher can formally administer a lesson-prompt every five or six weeks throughout the school year (at a maximum). The recommended classroom time allotment for each assessment is three hours: two hours for prewriting activities and one hour for students to write. Follow-up can extend from one or two hours (where students review the rubric and their scores, rewrite their papers, and rescore) to five or six hours or more (where students actually score each others' writing and practice applying the rubric). The extended follow-up has as much to do with teaching as with evaluating and is a powerful component.

A second way in which *Prompted to Write* can be used is at a grade level. Teachers administer the same prompt, score the essays collaboratively, and use results to gather information about student writing performance that puts the group's work in grade-level perspective. Teachers tell us repeatedly how community scoring events (grade-level and larger schoolwide scoring events) help them learn how their students are performing in relation to a larger group of students and help them gauge their teaching in relation to what's demanded of all students. An extensive explanation of the scoring process is provided in Chapter Five.

Finally, as suggested earlier, *Prompted to Write* can be the energizing basis of a schoolwide writing effort. Though it may seem odd to have all students in your school write to the same prompt and be evaluated on the same rubric, a schoolwide writing assessment reveals important (and often reassuring) information about student writing individually and at successive grades. We watched the results of schoolwide assessments over several years as student writing progressed from average scores of Nearly Proficient in sixth grade to Proficient in seventh grade to Commendable in eighth grade. The pattern was remarkable. With principal support and teacher buy-in, students understood that they were participating in an important activity that would (and did!) help them become better writers. Teachers looked forward to the scoring days and regarded them as important opportunities to connect with each other and discuss effective methods for teaching writing.

Finally, the lessons in *Prompted to Write* address standards through the scoring guides for each assessment. The rubrics identify and describe the particular writing skills necessary for Proficient or Commendable writing performance, and are aligned to specific skills delineated in writing standards across the country. We think you'll find the package that this book represents useful. It's what for years we wished we'd had as teachers, and we send it in your direction with excitement and passion.

Through postings on CATENet (thanks to Jim Burke), the scholarly work of George Hillocks, and support that the Bay Area Writing Project provides to expand and deepen our practice, we've learned that notwithstanding the increasing restrictions of mandated assessment systems and constant changes in educational priorities, writing can prevail. We must work hard to promote critical thinking through writing in the classroom—even when the emphasis and time demands of so many tests make the effort seem nearly impossible. Our years as educators have shown us that integrating quality authentic writing tests into a classroom, grade-level, or schoolwide writing program can drive whole-school reform, teacher collaboration, and student writing improvement in profound ways.

ACKNOWLEDGMENTS

We would like to thank our colleagues at Education Task Force and Marina Middle School for ongoing support as we've worked to refine writing and the teaching of writing in our communities. In particular, we're grateful to Beth Morton, Gretchen Muller, Dale Davidson, Carol Schauer, Rod Septka, Kim Suppes, Dyan Pike, and Dorie Yim. We'd also like to thank our friends and colleagues from ACCESS, who got us started with Writing Samples and large-scale assessments so many years ago. We continue to be connected to these wise and committed educators: Audrey Fielding, Marty Williams, and Marean Jordan. The Bay Area Writing Project, under the direction of Carol Tateishi, has given us ongoing opportunities to be "investigators of writing instruction" and to increase our understanding of the complexity of teaching and learning writing. We'd like to recognize these teachers for piloting the lessons and helping us fine-tune the prompts: Elf Diggerman, Victor Jacob, Steve Pederson, Mary K. Sayle, and Jennifer Gagan. These administrators were supportive throughout the book's development: Dennis Chew, Judy Giampaoli, and Paul Marcoux of Marina Middle School. We'd like to thank Robert Masolele. And finally, we are grateful to the students who have contributed their writing here; to Christie Hakim, our editor, for helping us shape a work that became much more than it was when we began; and to our families for their patience and encouragement all along the way: Alex and Sarah Baky, and Geraldine, Gabe, and Jessica Fleming.

Meredith Pike-Baky designs and delivers professional development workshops, works as a teacher-coach, and facilitates articulation between levels and schools in a variety of subjects. She is currently a curriculum and assessment coordinator in a consortium of eleven public school districts and a local community college, grades K–14, just north of San Francisco. *Prompted to Write* reflects nearly twenty years of her work in linking high-quality curriculum and assessment. Meredith started teaching in the Peace Corps in Togo, West Africa. She became interested in teaching writing as instructor of Subject A for Nonnative Speakers at UC Berkeley and went on to become part of ACCESS, a school reform project based on relevant and rigorous content in San Francisco middle schools. Her teaching and workshops have taken her to the Navajo Reservation, Egypt, Japan, Thailand, Taiwan, Turkey, and Costa Rica. Fortunately, her two college-age children love to travel as much as she does.

Gerald Fleming has taught in the San Francisco Public Schools for thirty-four years, and currently teaches at Marina Middle School. He was named Bay Area Middle School Teacher of the Year by San Francisco State University, served as a Mentor Teacher for over a decade, and serves on the District's Peer Assistance Review Board.

He's the author (with Meredith Pike-Baky) of *Rain, Steam, and Speed: Developing Fluency in Adolescent Writers,* and for five years edited and published the literary magazine *Barnabe Mountain Review.* Sixteen Rivers Press recently has issued a book of his poetry, *Swimmer Climbing onto Shore.*

PART ONE

Instructional Process

Bridging the Testing/Teaching Gap

Issues and Challenges

A writing teacher's dream:

You're in your classroom, surveying your thirty-or-so students busily revising their essays. They're working independently except for brief conversations when they gather in twos or threes to make sure a turn of phrase or transition or conclusion they've just added enhances the effectiveness of their essays. You've managed to build time into your schedule to allow three weeks for this project, and you've only stopped students from their writing to introduce some fresh prewriting activities (drawing, perhaps, or interviewing a classmate) and to review the form and function of a counterargument. You've had the luxury to spend time (during the daily hour reserved for writing) conferring with individual students about their drafts. This period is popular with your students, all of whom you've been able to engage—opening their writing to some interesting topics, coaching the hesitant writers via frequent mini-conferences. The sweetly oiled machine of your writers' workshop is humming smoothly.

If you've seen anything like this in real life, you're lucky. This vision of a classroom writing program that provides focused attention to individual writers seems a remote ideal for most of us. Faced with increasing demands to prepare students for high-stakes multiple choice tests and required to implement increasingly prescribed literacy programs (making *individual* instruction almost impossible), many teachers have had to abandon well-established, thematically driven, student-centered writing programs. We teachers have less time to craft instruction around current high-interest topics that motivate students to write. Instead, we feel compelled to prepare students for spontaneous writing in response to impersonal and generic topics, robbing them of opportunities to see the integral link between reading and writing, to develop their writing over multiple drafts, and to practice writing for different purposes. Students simply don't develop as writers.

Meaningful writing instruction has been shortchanged as assessment readiness has taken a lead role in many schools. Day after day of classroom instruction is spent on "drill and kill" test readiness booklets, force-feeding students, their eyes glazed, with information national or state bodies have deemed important.

The result? Writing programs almost everywhere have suffered. As states have adopted lists of standards and multiple choice tests, meaningful writing instruction has devolved into a series of fragmented assignments driven by testing priorities. Formerly student-centered, meaning-based instructional programs have been replaced by prescriptive textbook series or formulaic writing agendas, leaving little room for students to move in directions of their own interests and find their own voices, and still less room for teachers to branch off into areas of local or contemporary relevance. Such one-size-fits-all approaches to writing have become common in many districts nationwide. As a result of these conditions, we're already witnessing decreased student interest in writing as well as a diminished ability to use writing as a way to extend and deepen thinking. Students resist writing more than ever and do not have opportunities to practice (or see the value of) developing ideas over time. Test results in many states (both performance measures and standardized test scores) show increasingly lower results in writing.

WHY TEACH ASSESSMENT-BASED WRITING?

Are we advocating a test-free education? Not at all. Writing tests help monitor and improve our teaching, and they're also a reality for students applying to high schools or colleges, for scholarships, and, of course, for jobs. They're required components of many courses and of school and district exit exams, and we're witnessing a renewed emphasis on writing tests as a window into the thinking and problem-solving abilities of students at all ages across the curriculum.

Though they take different forms, writing assessments abound. Curriculum standards in all states identify narrative and expository writing types as priorities for instruction and assessment. These genres are tested in a variety of ways at many different levels. Sometimes the assessments serve as benchmarks to signify whether or not students are on track for meeting graduation or exit requirements. Sometimes they are the gates that permit students to pass to the next level, gain admission to a school, or demonstrate proficiency in a subject to circumvent a required class. In addition to local varieties of writing tests administered by schools, districts, and states, there are large-scale national writing tests. These are generally high-stakes assessments upon which important decisions are based. They're also used to monitor the writing performance of large groups of students, both in the United States and internationally. The College Board has recently replaced the analogies section of the SAT with a writing sample, and almost all states administer formal writing tests. What all have in common is the expectation that students will respond to a reading selection or series of questions by writing a substantive, coherent, correct essay in a limited amount of time.

We need to prepare students to perform at their highest levels in these situations. And, of course, many skills required on these tests are necessary for more than test-taking. Much writing is done under time constraints. The ability to write succinctly and spontaneously is important for conveying and recording information, communicating effectively, and demonstrating what the writer has learned or experienced. Writing on demand is a useful lifelong skill.

The dilemma that we as educators face is to know where instruction and assessment meet: that is, what the criteria are for assessments that not only measure student achievement but also enhance and promote real learning. Unfortunately, many tests are poorly designed; they're disconnected from students' lives and from what students learn in the classroom. Further, they fail to provide timely information that teachers or students can use.

Our challenge becomes daunting. How do we, teachers who believe in the power of writing and the attendant search for meaning in young students' lives, preserve a quality instructional program when external demands rob us of the necessary time and focus such a deep program requires? While nothing can replace a flexible, personalized, and process-oriented writing program, we *do* believe that it's possible to continue to implement a quality writing curriculum through a series of comprehensive, custom-designed performance assessments. Our years of curriculum coaching, performance assessment coordination, and teaching have shown us that integrating quality authentic writing tests into a classroom or a grade-level or schoolwide writing program can be powerful. It can drive whole-school reform, teacher collaboration, and student writing improvement in profound ways.

In such a program, students develop versatility, and they progress as writers while at the same time teachers gather data about the effectiveness of their instruction. *Prompted to Write* responds to the challenge writing teachers face by offering lessons that integrate into the current instructional context. These lessons will guide you and your students in a series of activities that develop literacy while engaging students' interest and simultaneously preparing them for on-demand writing tests.

WHAT IS EFFECTIVE WRITING INSTRUCTION?

Many teachers believe that students learn to write effectively by working through stages of the writing process. The purest form of this pedagogical model is Writer's Workshop, where students choose their own topics and move through brainstorming, organizing, drafting, and revising their writing to arrive at a final draft. In this model, the teacher and students develop a classroom culture of shared enthusiasm for writing, creating a safe environment in which to take risks while building respect for everyone's efforts. Teaching comes in the form of mini-lessons, short periods of direct instruction targeting particular aspects of writing reflective of the specific genre, topic, or area with which students are struggling. Student writers share their writing by reading progressive drafts from the "Author's Chair" and getting feedback from classmates about what listeners (and readers) like about the piece and where questions remain. Writer's Workshop builds confidence and commitment in student writers and can yield exceptional student writing. For teachers with much to teach, however, the downside of Writer's Workshop is that writing projects take weeks to complete.

Colleagues from what we consider the opposite end of the continuum believe that practice with one-liner prompts teaches spontaneous writing and prepares students for the large-scale assessments they face in the spring. Repeated practice at spontaneous writing in isolation doesn't really *teach* writing, of course, though it may help students identify topics on which they write easily, and it may ultimately reduce test anxiety. Absent from this model is any instruction in writing strategies, attention to the stages of the writing process that give students planning time, or techniques for organizing an effective piece of writing. Students come away from these one-liner prompt exercises lacking a sense that writing is an organic process, that it germinates from the seed of an idea, grows, and, with proper nourishment and deft pruning, flourishes. And, of course, one-liners can—in a single tyrannical line—devastate student confidence when their victims are unable to respond to them.

How can we connect both ends of this writing instruction continuum? The response is to give students—via interesting, well-developed, process-oriented prompts—practice at moving through the writing process in the limited amount of time that is the reality in most of our schools. We also must create opportunities for students to build a repertoire of writing strategies and develop the versatility to write for a variety of purposes. To extend and develop their ideas, students need time to think about and talk about their ideas. The prompt-lessons in *Prompted to Write* offer a middle ground, a meeting place if you will, for all of us working to teach meaningful writing in the context of large-scale standards-aligned assessments.

Writing Instruction Continuum

Writer's Workshop: Students choose their topics and move through several revisions, taking time to peer counsel and meet with teacher. Instruction is focused in mini-lessons.

Test-Prep Model: Students write on demand to a series of very brief prompts, increasing readiness for standardized tests.

$\longleftrightarrow$

Prompted to Write offers a middle ground for teachers working to bridge extreme approaches in writing instruction.

The *Prompted to Write* Model
Preparing Students to Do Their Best

Each of the lessons in *Prompted to Write* follows a predictable structure. The lesson activities correspond to stages of the writing process. They shepherd students through prewriting, drafting, revising, editing, and publishing. There are variations from lesson to lesson depending on the writing type and the topic, steering students' attention toward the purpose and audience of each assignment. For each lesson, students have an opportunity to

- Connect their own knowledge and experiences to the writing topic (build schema).
- Read with, listen to, and talk with classmates to expand their thinking on the topic.
- Generate relevant vocabulary through guided exercises.
- Consider the purpose of the writing task and the audience, adjusting formality and selecting vocabulary appropriately.
- Plan and organize their ideas for writing.
- Revise and edit their writing by reviewing a checklist.
- Compare their writing strengths and weaknesses to descriptors on the scoring guide and to student examples.
- If teachers choose to use class essays as instructional tools, compare models of peer writing at various proficiency levels.

STRUCTURED PREWRITING ACTIVITIES

Each prompt-lesson in this book embeds preparation for the writing task by presenting a series of activities, each progressing gradually from familiar to unfamiliar, easy to difficult, simple to complex, culminating with the writing assignment itself and its assessment. The writing is a synthesis of what students have practiced and prepared for. For example, students identify related experiences, learn associated vocabulary, observe another writer's organization of ideas, and trade reactions to a reading selection with a classmate. Through such activities, students become fluent in the topic before they have to write and are much better equipped to do well than if they were simply given their prompt cold. This breaking down of one complex task (the final writing assignment) into smaller discrete skills is referred to, as you know, as *scaffolded instruction*. Each prompt-lesson in *Prompted to Write* is carefully scaffolded, and the figurative scaffold itself is easy for teachers to visualize and understand.

In addition, a scoring guide (a *holistic rubric*) is included with every lesson so that teachers can present the expectations for student writing in explicit terms. Students can refer to the scoring guide at the beginning of the prewriting section, midway through, or immediately before writing the essay itself. Giving students the opportunity to understand and internalize expectations for their writing helps them write more skillfully. Annotated student examples representing a range of writing types in response to selected prompts are included in Appendix A. The student examples translate the features of the rubric into real student writing. Presenting clear descriptions and student examples makes learning—and subsequent improvement—tangible and therefore vastly easier than would be possible without these supports. The goal, ultimately, is to have characteristics of excellent essays become second nature for each student—each not only conversant with rubric characteristics but also able to integrate them into dynamic essays.

Activities are customized to prepare students for the particular writing challenges of each lesson. For example, a drawing exercise helps students develop their abilities to describe in Lesson 1, "A Personal Oasis." In Lesson 11, "Junk Food Lunches?," a planning outline guides the organization of ideas for a persuasive essay. In Lesson 14, "Unlikely Thieves," a T-chart helps students address opposing points of view in an argument essay, and in Lesson 12, "Key to Success," where students write a speech, they are encouraged to think of a familiar expression or proverb to introduce their main idea.

In addition to the diverse activities, the lesson activities vary the ways students respond within an activity. For example, students react to a reading selection orally and in small groups, complete a prewriting chart, attempt an illustration or write dialogue to organize ideas, and take time to edit as they complete their first draft. By moving through the writing process in a compressed period of time, by exercising all language skills (listening, speaking, reading, writing), and by using multiple learning modes and styles, students are both interested and motivated, so they tend to perform at their highest level.

QUALITY WRITING PROMPTS

In the vernacular of today's schools, *prompts* are writing test topics. Prompts themselves are departure points to get students writing. They come long and short, sometimes attached to cryptic quotes, paired with literary excerpts, or as stand-alones. They can sometimes be remote from students' experiences (even preposterous) or so general that they're mortifyingly boring and students find themselves hard-pressed to respond with engagement or enthusiasm. Good writing tests begin with good prompts.

There's an art to designing successful prompts. Just as in high-quality instructional units, prompts must tap student interests. They must provide a focus that offers critical thinking opportunities. They must be written to a real, living, breathing, life-experiencing reader. A study conducted alongside the 1998 National Assessment of Educational Progress writing exam points to three critical components of well-crafted writing prompts: a balance between too much and too little information in the assignment, a topic that engages students in complex thinking, and an authentic audience. *Prompted to Write* honors each of these components.

Finally, good writing prompts generate important information about individual students that few other vehicles provide. That information can show us individual student progress and enable us to further refine instruction based on score results. When writing prompts reflect instruction, they link learning and testing and make the time spent on assessment not just worthwhile but richly valuable.

More and more, teachers are trying to design or request prompts that engage students and meet them at their developmental levels to enable the best snapshot of their writing and thinking. Obviously, since student interest and ability levels are so varied (even in the most homogeneous of classrooms), good prompts must be focused but at the same time open enough to allow for multiple departure points, to allow students' bright, individual selves to shine through. They're best when they revolve around current, relevant topics and embed a series of activities that galvanize students to *want* to write. Students need time, even in an on-demand writing test, to think and talk and read and plan. They need to generate vocabulary, remember relevant experiences, and figure out how they really do feel and what they really do think about a particular controversial issue as they get ready to write.

Good prompts are also characterized by what they produce. Direct, authentic, process-conscious writing tests yield diverse and lively writing interesting for teachers (and other students!) to read. In addition, good prompts make student performance expectations explicit by providing rubrics or scoring guides and samples of scored student work. Finally,

---

Good Prompts

- Engage
- Are focused
- Are relevant
- Integrate all skills
- Allow for various approaches
- Are explicit about expectations
- Are developmentally appropriate
- Produce diverse and lively writing
- Offer a snapshot of a student's best writing
- Provide important information about learning and teaching

---

instructionally sound prompts provide important information about group and individual student progress for both students and teachers.

In addition to honoring interesting topics, prompts must be accessible to both boys and girls. From many years of designing, implementing, and evaluating writing assessments, working with teachers, interviewing students, and administering hundreds of writing assessments, we've found that in general, prompts that boys can relate to girls relate to as well. The opposite, however, is *not* true. Boys have a more difficult time relating to prompts and topics that we know girls favor. Therefore, sensitivity to gender preferences is critical in designing prompts that will produce earnest writing—a sensitivity that, no matter what gender predilections exist, can appeal equally to either boys or girls.

TIMED WRITING PRACTICE

To be able to write under time constraints, students must practice. The lessons here provide multiple genres and topics with accompanying scaffolded activities to move students toward greater confidence and improved skills in writing on demand. We have designed the lessons so that students will generally spend twice as much time preparing to write (reading, thinking, talking, planning) as they spend writing.

HOLISTIC ASSESSMENT

Just as a classroom, grade-level, or schoolwide writing assessment program can act as the centerpiece of a writing curriculum, the measurement tool, the *rubric*, is the core of a particular assignment. A rubric, or scoring guide (and we use these terms interchangeably throughout the book), is a list of features used to establish standards and evaluate a piece of writing. The features describe and distinguish different levels of writing, though we rarely find a one-to-one correspondence between a piece of writing and the set of descriptors for a particular score point level. The best rubrics are objective and specific: they use unambiguous language easy for students to understand, and they're specific to a particular assignment. The best rubrics give students concrete and specific ways to improve their writing and use language that is descriptive rather than judgmental (for example, using *Developing* rather than *Minimal* for Score Point 1). It's nearly impossible for teachers to find or generate rubrics for every project they assign, and the market has responded by offering a variety of "generic rubrics." These are rubrics that do it all and are used to score numerous different assignments, and unsurprisingly they vary in quality and effectiveness.

We believe that *holistic* rubrics respond best to the complexity of a piece of writing. Any piece of writing is complex. Consider for a minute the many components to even the simplest writing. For example, there's the writer's perspective and opinions; the level of directness with which the writer approaches the topic; the writer's vocabulary and syntax; the way in which ideas are presented, organized, defended, and explained; and the general control of language, the voice, both rhetorically and grammatically.

However, to reach large groups of students, sometimes teachers (and texts) focus on only a few concrete elements. These may be organization (paragraphing, sequencing of ideas) or correctness (grammar, punctuation, spelling) or even elements such as titles, margins, and handwriting. These elements are easier to identify and often easier to teach than more complex components such as development of ideas, elaboration of opinion, and voice. Focusing on the tangible and (some say) superficial elements of a piece of writing unfortunately conveys to students that form is more important than content in writing. Students in these classes don't learn that a piece of writing is, above all, an exercise in conveying ideas. Teaching students the interplay between the components of a piece of writing is challenging, and takes a different direction, of course, depending on the assignment's purpose and audience. Therefore, a complex piece of writing, we hope, is most honestly addressed and judiciously assessed when regarded not as a collection of skills viewed in isolation but as a whole.

A holistic rubric addresses the complexity of writing by identifying the most important features of a particular piece of writing while giving teachers guidelines for prioritizing and evaluating them. Unlike an *analytic rubric,* which evaluates each writing feature in isolation, a *holistic rubric* scores a piece of writing based on the sum of its features. Two pieces of writing could thus receive the same score for addressing an assignment in completely different ways. And while analytic evaluation is what we as educators are trained to do, it's inadequate for judging writing. Analytic evaluation conveys to students an artificial message: it breaks a piece of writing into separate, isolated components, and it doesn't help students see how the components work together to form a compelling whole.

Holistic evaluation focuses on strengths of a piece of writing rather than on weaknesses, so writers get credit for what they do best. While we want students to develop all the skills writing requires (organization, elaboration, lively and specific language, correctness in conventions, voice), we're *also* aware that student writers not only develop at different speeds, they excel in different areas. We ought to acknowledge a piece of student writing with nearly perfect language control but not much voice or engagement in writing just as we ought to reward writing that has lots of voice and enthusiasm but is a little wild in language control. After all, a teacher's goal is holistic, too, isn't it? We want to draw out the unique voice of each student writer while teaching standard conventions and tricks of the trade. A holistic rubric supports such goals.

Rubrics have been customized to set student goals and provide the teacher (or student!) evaluation criteria for the particular genre and topic. Though each of the fifteen rubrics include the elements of idea development, organization, and language and mechanics, each is specially tailored for specific prompts. All the rubrics in *Prompted to Write* are intended to be applied holistically. They identify guidepost features for instruction and writing. The four score-point levels describe each feature in specific terms. Student examples are included in Appendix A to further clarify the meaning of each of the score points and to give you a sense of real-world anchoring.

Understanding and Teaching the Lessons

Each lesson in *Prompted to Write* includes these parts:

- Getting Started
- Reading
- Thinking and Talking
- Planning Activity (sometimes combined with "Thinking and Talking")
- Writing Prompt
- Revising and Editing Checklist
- Self-Assessment
- Scoring Guide

Each lesson begins with an introduction, alerting students to the general subject of the prompt, then moves to "Getting Started," an activity wherein students identify first thoughts or previous experiences related to the general topic. This is *schema building,* and we know that by encouraging students to connect old and new material we increase both their engagement and their opportunity to excel. Sometimes students draw as part of this activity, sometimes they talk with classmates, and sometimes they jot notes. In these ways, they're accessing and building schema, the personal set of skills and knowledge each student brings to the task.

The next phase of the lesson, the "Reading," features a passage (often an excerpt from the work of a well-known writer) that models the writing assignment and presents one approach. The passage presents ideas and vocabulary related to the topic and provides time for students to deepen their understanding of and reflect on past experiences with the topic. It often suggests different but related departure points for student writing.

In "Thinking and Talking," classmates discuss what they've read through an activity that sets them up for the writing task. This activity is usually done in small groups, but can be done individually. Sometimes it's an analysis of the structure of the selection, leading students to organize their own ideas similarly. Sometimes it's a series of questions, highlighting particularly effective features of what they read and suggesting that students try out those same writing strategies.

The "Planning" section of each lesson guides students to think out their writing. They're encouraged to elaborate on early ideas, go back to the reading selection for examples of techniques, or develop and expand answers to questions. *Expansion* is key here, for it lays the groundwork for what's soon to come.

The "Writing Prompt" is the fuel that drives the rest of the process; it's a reiteration of the task (sometimes offering a range of options). It galvanizes students to synthesize activities they've already completed in order to write their best.

"Revising and Editing" gives students a checklist with which to review and quickly revise their writing. They're guided to check development and elaboration of their ideas. They're also alerted to particular features of the writing type. The checklist is intended to teach students the habit of revising and editing even in an on-demand writing context. (The whole writing process *is* possible even within a limited time period!) At the end of the checklist, students have an opportunity to evaluate their writing *based on previous experience with the scoring guide.* (If the students have not yet reviewed the scoring guide, this step is not recommended.)

Each lesson includes a "Scoring Guide" section for teachers (or, again, students—and we discuss this at length later) tailored to the specific writing task. The "Scoring Guide" is an evaluation tool describing four levels of writing performance; it is intended to be used by both teachers and students. The description of each performance level corresponds to categories or features of the particular writing type. These guides can (and we think *should*) be used as teaching tools as well as for evaluation. Teachers can use specific rubric features (such as *Clarity of Position and Support of Argument* or *Audience Awareness*) to plan instruction and target individual student support. Training students to apply the scoring guides to their own and each other's writing is an effective way of helping them internalize characteristics of excellent writing.

While the individual features of each scoring guide help teachers target instruction, they shouldn't be used in isolation when scoring. As we've discussed earlier, each rubric is intended to evaluate student writing holistically, as the sum of its components rather than as an evaluation of the separate components. It's important for teachers and students to practice and understand holistic scoring before applying the scoring guides in these lessons. A detailed explanation of how to use the scoring guides is presented in Part One: Chapters Five and Six.

Nine "Student Exemplars" are included in Appendix A, and two more in Chapter Five. They show pieces demonstrating each of four levels of performance. Student examples are probably the most powerful tools for rendering the complex mosaic of a piece of writing real and concrete to students. We've found that vivid student examples bring an otherwise abstract set of scoring criteria to life. They help students see that proficient and commendable writing *is* possible. Some teachers use student examples effectively by introducing them at the beginning of the lesson rather than at the end. Several suggestions for using student examples appear in Chapter Six.

The examples we've chosen have been selected because each includes most of the rubric's features for the corresponding score point. Many are middle school examples, and high school students certainly will produce more sophisticated writing—and more nuanced variations of score-point features—in their higher-end essays.

STAGING AND TIMING A LESSON FROM *PROMPTED TO WRITE*

Since *Prompted to Write* provides practice in on-demand writing, timing the different sections of a lesson is important. Experience has taught us that the ratio of two to one (two parts prewriting to one part writing) is realistic for what students need and for what's demanded of them on writing tests and in subsequent job application situations. The prompts here are designed to be completed in three hours of class time: two hours for prewriting activities and one hour for writing, revising, and editing. The three hours can be distributed over one, two, or three days.

The structure of each lesson-prompt is designed to be easy to follow for both teachers and students. We recommend introducing each section sequentially as it appears, presenting the rubric after students have become familiar with the rhythm of the lesson. We've provided timing guidelines, leaving flexibility for the teacher to adjust timing according to the needs of specific groups of students.

The following section presents an overview of the time line. It will serve as a starting point for covering an entire lesson-prompt in the recommended three hours.

THE INSTRUCTIONAL PROCESS

The following step-by-step guide is how we've found it best to proceed when teaching a lesson.

Prewriting Activities

- Introduce the task and the topic.

- Have students orally and briefly share previous knowledge and experiences related to the topic.

- Set a supportive tone in order to lower anxiety about timed writing.

- Have students complete the "Getting Started" section individually; those who want to can share their work.

- Introduce and set up the reading selection: give background about author and subject; ask students to share their previous experience with either.

- Read the selection: you can read it aloud or have a skilled student or series of students do so, or students can read silently. (We prefer the first option initially, having found that we can ensure classwide comprehension through oral reading and teacher interpretation.)

- Have students work in pairs to complete activities in the "Talking and Thinking" section. Review and validate responses.

This is the end of the first hour of the first day. You may need to adjust the timing if your students need more time on this step or if your classes are less than sixty minutes long.

Planning Support

- Briefly review and refresh key points from the "Getting Started," "Reading," and "Talking and Thinking" sections. Explain and assign the "Planning" section, modeling the activity first. (Give students the option of using their own paper or of completing this activity on an available computer.) Move around the classroom coaxing and coaching reluctant writers to get started and encouraging students to work together to develop their ideas.

- Present the rubric. Read it through with students and clarify features. Ask students to point out examples of rubric features from the reading selection. Show your admiration if they can do so.

- Either read orally or have students read (again, orally or silently) a student example. Compare the score the student example received with the rubric description itself. Elicit from students, if you can, specific examples of connections between the essay score and the specific rubric description. Encourage the use of language from the rubric.

- Talk with and prepare students for the next step, the writing task, and encourage them to bring notes from the prewriting activities and to allot their time wisely. Tell them that they will work independently during the writing.

This is the end of the second hour and perhaps the second day; adjust timing appropriately.

The Writing Assignment

- Have students clear their desks of everything except their materials for the writing task: pen or pencils, computer, prompt packet (including Scoring Guide), and notes.

- Alert students to the "Revising and Editing Checklist."

- Have students write their names on their papers according to your system (refer to the next section, "Labeling the Papers.")

- Go over the writing prompt, reading it aloud, interpreting it, making sure that students understand it.

- Launch student writing, insisting on the quiet necessary for concentrated work, and move around the classroom for the first few minutes, encouraging writers to sustain momentum and leave time for rereading and minor revisions.

- Give students a little warning at the final ten-minute and five-minute points, and have them turn in their writing at the end of this hour.

This concludes the lesson. Later chapters discuss ways to proceed with the papers.

LABELING THE PAPERS

Before students begin their writing, you will want to decide and tell them how they should identify their papers. It's important to keep papers anonymous to maintain reliability during scoring. Student writing can be identified and submitted in either of these ways, the less desirable discussed first:

- *On binder paper:* Students write on one side of each page, recording their name, teacher, class, and period number and date on the back of the last page, upside down at the bottom. This is the quicker, less expensive option. (It's also, unfortunately, the more difficult to read en masse, because of little irritants like different-sized paper and varying line size.)

- *On a preprinted form:* The best version of this we've used is included as Appendix D of this book. It is an 11" by 17" sheet folded in half with lines for student writing on four pages. (You can also use two 8.5" by 11" plain paper sheets.) At the top of the first page is a header (this can be something like "Writing to a Prompt," "Writing Sample," or "Timed Writing") with adequate space for the student's own title. In the top right corner are three circles for first, second, and if necessary third reading scores. On the back of the last page, upside down at the bottom (to discourage scorers from peeking at names) is a box wherein students each write their name, teacher, class and period number, and date, and a smaller box in which scorers enter the average (final) score. This option looks more formal and official than binder paper and is useful for students who need such structural prodding to be motivated, and it allows students to collect their on-demand writing in a tidy file. This form also makes mass scorings infinitely easier than random-sized—and often ragged-edged—binder paper sheets. If scorers feel that no student names should be visible—even upside down—removable stickers (available inexpensively in office supply stores) can be used to cover student names for either of these options.

INTRODUCING THE RUBRIC AND USING STUDENT EXAMPLES

It has become common practice in many classrooms to use rubrics with students to build an understanding of the expectations of many different activities before students perform them. The rubrics in *Prompted to Write* are written to be used by both teachers and students. Some teachers present the rubric at the outset of the lesson, while others wait to present the rubric when students get ready to write. In either case, students learn what their writing will be evaluated on *before* they write. When expectations are explicit, students have a better chance of performing at a higher level.

We recommend presenting the rubric through each feature, having one student read aloud the description at each level. In other words, in presenting the "Scoring Guide for Lesson 1: A Personal Oasis" (Writing About a Place, on page 64), Student #1 would read what "Description" looks like at a 4, 3, 2, and 1 level. Student #2 would do the same with the next feature, in this case, "Organization of Ideas." Move through the rubric slowly and clearly, asking students to explain words others don't understand and pointing out the differences in features from level to level.

What if you (or your students) want to modify the rubric? This is great if it makes the scoring guide more concrete or specific to the students' needs. You can substitute words or change descriptors. And since the number of score-point levels on a rubric should reflect the levels at which your students write, you can even add a higher level: a "5" (for *Exceptional, Extraordinary Achievement*) if you think there is at least one student who can write at that level, either now or sometime during the school year.

However, we caution against modifying the rubric so that it becomes a checklist. As we've explained earlier, checklists are not effective in capturing, rewarding, or acknowledging the complexity of a piece of writing. The value of holistic rubrics is that they honor the complexity of writing and multiple ways different writers can approach such complexity. Even the most emerging writers can appreciate and learn from that.

General Tips for Succeeding with a Lesson

- Except in writing the essay itself, encourage students to work with partners as often as possible. Students learn from each other; they're more engaged when they can share ideas. Furthermore, talking about ideas before writing about them helps students clarify, expand, and extend those ideas. Talking about writing is what writers often do.

- Hold fast to time limits. It might take the class a session or two to become accustomed to these limits, but in this way students learn to discipline themselves carefully. They practice organizing their time in order to complete their writing. They practice strategies to lower anxiety during writing tests.

- Provide folders in which students can collect all the writing connected to the lessons. Students can observe their growth as writers and perhaps choose a timed writing piece to expand and develop for a subsequent assignment.

VARIATIONS ON MOVING THROUGH THE LESSONS

While the sequence of each of the lessons is designed to provide effective instructional scaffolding for students so that they can write their best when they arrive at the prompt, it's possible to vary the sequence of prompt lessons to address particular needs. Here are some ways you may want to vary the lessons:

- Introduce the rubric at the beginning of the lesson, explaining its features with as many concrete examples as possible.

- Introduce the rubric and a student example at the beginning of a lesson.

- Design a mini-lesson on a rubric feature. (Two handouts, "Narrative Writing Strategies" [Appendix B] and "Persuasive Writing Pitfalls" [Appendix C] are starting points for mini-lessons.)

- Substitute a "Student Exemplar" or a piece of writing from one of your previous students or another selection for the "Reading." Remember that this selection should model the task students do in the "Writing" phase of the lesson.

- Share your own writing (of the same writing type on a related topic) with students to experience some of the challenges students face, to demonstrate that you value what they're being assigned, and to suggest some additional writing strategies.

Extending the Writing Time

If you find that students for the most part have impressively been on task for the period and that a goodly number of them ask for more time when you pose the question at the end of the period, why not give them more time—a fixed, announced amount—if your schedule the next day allows for it? (Two notes here: First, the continuation *must* occur the next day if students are to remain focused on the topic. Second, if you're doing a grade-level or schoolwide writing, *all* staff must agree to the same protocol in issues like these if the community assessment is to be fair and valid.

Writing Outside Class

We dislike this idea, having tried it, having seen its effects. Here's what happens: Students take the unfinished essay from your classroom. Yes, some *do* simply take them home and sit quietly at an uncluttered desk under an adequate lamp and write for the prescribed amount of time, but *others* (alas, *many* others) do one or more of the following things: take it to lunch and work on it with friends, take it home and either intentionally or passively allow older brothers or sisters (or even parents!) to "consult" with them on it (usually resulting in an essay inferior to the one they themselves would have written), and, finally, *lose it,* therefore annihilating days of work.

So: if it's to be continued, the work should stay in your classroom until tomorrow.

Use of Dictionaries

We've found that the use of dictionaries, while an admirable impulse and resulting in somewhat fewer misspellings, is both a waste of precious time for the student and, if students are standing up to get or put back dictionaries, a distraction. The teacher's directions regarding spelling, then: simply encourage students to spell as well as they can, but not to get hung up (and therefore slowed *down*) in struggling over spelling.

Weaving the Lessons into a Year-Long Writing Program

Prompted to Write provides opportunities for students to hone their ability to write on demand in response to a range of issues for a variety of purposes. Our aim is to deepen the dynamics of on-demand writing—not only to serve you as a teacher but also to serve schools, districts, and, what is most important, students' living, breathing interests.

WRITING GENRES AND PURPOSES

The book's fifteen prompts include these specific writing types: personal description, personal narration, focused biography, narrative, response to literature, response to poetry, information, persuasion, and problem solution. Through this variety, students receive practice with genres most commonly taught and most frequently assessed. Some prompts ask students to write about real remembered experiences (Lesson 4, "Something I'll Never Forget") or imaginary places (Lesson 1, "A Personal Oasis"). While we know that most students find writing about real-life events most compelling, test prompts in some states sometimes feature fanciful or imaginary scenarios as prompts. Prompted to Write provides opportunities for students to practice both reality-based and imaginative writing. The "Key to Success" lesson, number 12, invites students to write and deliver a speech.

You can have your students write to a variety of narrative departure points. "Something I'll Never Forget" (Lesson 4), "A Childhood Passion" (Lesson 2), "Lucky Breaks" (Lesson 7), or "A Personal Hero" (Lesson 6) are some examples. Two interpretive prompts give students a chance to connect with and explain the meaning of a literature selection or a poem. An information-process task asks students to describe and extol a consumer item or service of interest. Finally, five prompts feature persuasive writing. These range from local issues (Lesson 11, "Junk Food Lunches?") to controversies of a more public nature (Lesson 14, "Unlikely Thieves").

The fifteen lessons in Prompted to Write are divided into three sections: "Writing to Discover and Reveal," "Writing to Inform and Explain," and "Writing to Support a Claim." Each lesson follows a similar sequence, moving through stages of the writing process. The

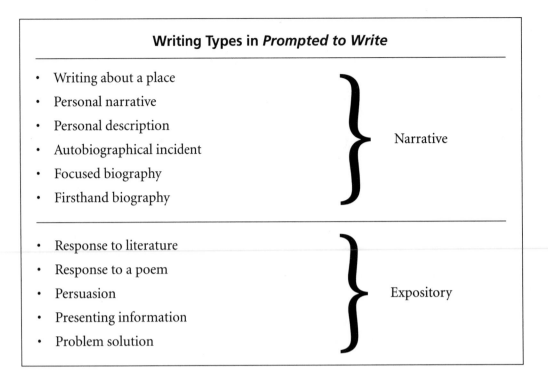

Writing Types in *Prompted to Write*

- Writing about a place
- Personal narrative
- Personal description
- Autobiographical incident
- Focused biography
- Firsthand biography

} Narrative

- Response to literature
- Response to a poem
- Persuasion
- Presenting information
- Problem solution

} Expository

fifteen lessons move student writing from narrative to exposition. The writing types and purposes parallel the important "personal-to-public" progression by beginning with personal narrative and taking student writing to sophisticated persuasion. Over the course of a school year, teachers can have students move through the book sequentially, or they can choose to cycle recursively through the book by selecting one prompt in each section, then returning to the first section after completing the cycle. This latter option is our preference; it keeps the writing types fresh (students and teachers benefit from variety, no?) and gives students a chance to return to a familiar genre after they've experimented with something different.

Research and experience have taught us that students learn most effectively when they begin with what they know and care about—even if their experience and knowledge are neither wide nor deep. With that in mind, the prompts in *Prompted to Write* follow these progressions:

- Familiar → New
- Personal → Public
- Concrete → Abstract

This sequence enables you to validate students' knowledge and skills and (by beginning with topics that invite students to share information about themselves) establishes a tone of support and enthusiasm for what they bring to the classroom. While there's an overall progression from easy to difficult across the fifteen lessons, the prompts within each of the three sections also progress from easy to difficult. In other words, the prompts at the beginning of each section ("A Personal Oasis," "A Personal Hero," and "Junk Food Lunches?") are relatively easy and more accessible to students. They require less sophisticated critical thinking skills and writing strategies than those at the end of each section, "House on Fire," "Here's Something Cool!," and "Time to Go Alternative?"

By following this topic and genre progression, classroom communities can build trust and skills while experiencing a modified version of Writer's Workshop. (We don't have to sacrifice our commitment to the writing process, for these lessons can integrate *both* process *and* assessment!) By sharing personal preferences and experiences, students get to know each other. They collaborate on activities that collectively develop their writing skills. With consistent practice, they emerge prepared for the timed writing tests that abound throughout high school and for entrance into college and the workplace.

In addition, because the prompts within each section are different, you can select a prompt most appropriate for the interests and abilities of your students. If your students are emerging writers, for example, you may want to select "A Personal Oasis" and reserve "Something About Me You May Not Know" for more experienced writers or for later in the year.

Prompts we assign students should also take into account what we as teachers are passionate about. You know from experience in the classroom that when we're asking students to explore subjects and processes we find compelling, our energy increases and our enthusiasm transfers to students. Therefore, choose prompts that reflect *your* interests as well. If you'd like to expand student awareness of the environmental impact of SUVs, for example, you may want to select "Time to Go Alternative?" (Lesson 15) relatively early in the year. Or if you want to emphasize community building in your classroom by supporting students in sharing information about themselves, you can select "A Childhood Passion" (Lesson 2), "Something About Me You May Not Know" (Lesson 3), or "House on Fire" (Lesson 5).

Consider the following checklist when making choices about the lessons you want to feature:

- ☐ Your students' ability levels
- ☐ Standards and genres you'd like to address
- ☐ Your students' interests
- ☐ Your own preferences, interests, and passions
- ☐ What student writing topics you'll most enjoy reading

HOW TO WEAVE *PROMPTED TO WRITE* INTO YOUR YEAR-LONG WRITING PROGRAM

As mentioned earlier, we recommend cycling through each prompt section over the course of the school year to give students repeated experiences with each of the different genres. As Richard Sterling, director of the National Writing Project, points out, a single occasion of writing does not give a complete picture of a student's writing ability. Therefore, it's important to give students multiple opportunities to write, both for the invaluable practice it offers them and to provide a more complete picture of writing ability.

Of the fifteen writing lessons in *Prompted to Write,* you can select as many as eight to administer as formal on-demand writing snapshots over the course of the school year. Since each lesson doubles as a teaching unit, you need not fear you're sacrificing instruction to assessment. You can use lessons you didn't select as formal assessments to offer as additional writing opportunities, packets for homework, or independent study. Further, some can be reserved for grade-level or schoolwide assessments.

Evaluating Student Writing (and Teaching Students to Score)

Y ou've worked hard to teach a lesson in which students have produced their best writing in a limited time period. Your students are becoming familiar with writing under time pressure. How to proceed? Fortunately, what comes next has *no* time constraints—except, of course, your own desire to return papers soon enough for their writers to both remember them (!) and be motivated to learn from the results. In fact, what happens after the students have written can be the most powerful writing instruction you deliver. Using the results of one spontaneous writing opportunity to teach particular strategies as well as to prepare for the next on-demand prompt emphasizes the importance of scheduling several of these throughout the school year. But first, the writing must be scored. What we recommend here, we hope, will be useful for teachers, students, administrators, and even parents who may be called upon to participate in scoring.

UNDERSTANDING THE RUBRICS AND APPLYING THEM HOLISTICALLY

With a clear understanding of how student writing is evaluated, you can teach to expected outcomes and link your instruction explicitly to a rubric. This sets students up for success. But using a rubric and applying it holistically is neither intuitive for many of us nor easy the first time, so it's worth reviewing why and how to score holistically. Because writing is so complex—because it communicates ideas and reflects the various approaches, perspectives, and ability levels of our students—and because there are multiple ways a writer can tackle a topic effectively, we need a filter to help sift out what each student writer does best and where there are weaknesses. A good piece of writing is like a mosaic; writers arrange the components in unique ways. By taking a piece of writing as a whole and evaluating it on its strongest features, we're respecting the writer and doing justice to the complexity of writing.

Looking at the whole of a student paper, rather than approaching it as a series of separate skills, honors the work for what it is: an attempt at authentic communication of ideas.

Rubric Tip Sheet

Pages 27 and 28 show a glossary of terms that we've included to help you and your students demystify some of the secrets of good writing. You'll see these terms on the rubrics. Consider keeping this tip sheet handy for all the writing students do.

The Scoring Process

Scoring student writing involves reviewing the rubric, reading each paper, and determining a holistic score (a whole number) that corresponds to a score point reflecting most of the features. This process is most reliable if done twice, with each paper read by two different scorers. The final score is the average of the first two scores. If the difference between the two is more than one point, either a third scorer reads the paper and determines the final score or the first two scorers discuss their scores and rationale, coming to agreement through their discussion. Unfortunately, teachers often don't have a second reader to "read behind," so in this chapter, we'll describe how to score essays on your own for the students in your classes. In Chapter Six, we'll describe the steps for organizing a large-scale (and really worthwhile) multi-classroom scoring.

Classroom Evaluation: Scoring Your Students' Papers

Most teachers are familiar with holistic scoring. What we lay out for you here reflects what we've found to be the most reliable and efficient process. We hope you agree.

Drop your biases. Cast aside personal preferences for items not explicitly identified and described on the rubric. That's hard to do sometimes, but important. Beautiful handwriting is one example of a teacher's personal preference that will need to be suspended for a little while; a *terrific* essay might come from the hand of a student whose scribbles can be torturous to read. Conversely, an essay crafted in the best D'Nealian script may *look* good but possess few characteristics of excellence.

Try to come to each piece of writing fresh, without bringing knowledge of individual students' strengths and challenges. This way, you'll give each paper an objective read. Assuming that papers are anonymous (and this is important), resist the temptation to identify students' work from their handwriting. Be open to discovering new strengths (and new goals) for your students. Additional biases not mentioned in the rubrics that you'll want to abandon for scoring are length of papers (sometimes, but not necessarily, related to quality) or a particular political stance (the goal is clear, developed, and well-supported opinions, no matter what they are).

Reread the rubric. Even if you've read it many times, even if you *wrote* the rubric, reread it. Remind yourself of the features and the particular descriptors for each feature. Finally, make the shift from using the rubric for instruction to using the rubric for holistic evaluation. This means you want to prepare yourself to look for a *preponderance of evidence* corresponding to a score point rather than look for specific evidence for each feature of a score point. Refer to the "Rubric Tip Sheet" to refresh yourself on new terminology.

Rubric Tip Sheet

Here are some brief definitions of words used in improving and evaluating writing. Sometimes *knowing* the words—their concepts—paves the road toward better writing.

Analytic	Having to do with analysis.
Anchor Papers	A single set of scored student essays to link student writing to descriptors on the rubric; these keep the scorer *anchored* to consistent standards.
Anecdote	A little entertaining story.
Argument	Point of view or reason to support one's opinion.
Audience	The people reading the essay.
Audience Awareness	How writers anticipate what readers believe and answer questions or support their own point of view based on this prediction.
Behavior	The way someone acts in any given situation.
Benchmark	A reference point or indicator or standard in judging quality.
Clever	Showing quick or witty or sharp intelligence.
Commendable	Good; better than acceptable.
Conventions	Grammar, spelling, capitalization, and punctuation rules that writers follow.
Descriptive Strategies	Techniques writers use to describe a person, place, object, or event; they include sensory details, figurative language (similes and metaphors), use of images, anecdotes.
Develop	To become gradually better or stronger.
Dialogue	Talk between two or more people.
Diction	Language choice (vocabulary and sentences) used by the writer.
Disaggregate	To pull things apart or break them down in order to study the pieces and how they go together.
Distracting	Making a person think of something else besides the topic that is supposed to be under consideration.
Elaboration	How writers explain, develop, and support their ideas.
Engaging	Interesting, magnetic.
Errors	Mistakes.
Evidence	Experiences, reasons, examples that support an idea.
Exemplars	Examples.
Fitting Conclusion	A conclusion that emphasizes the main idea and ties together the essay.
General	Not specific or precise.
Generate	To make or create.
Holistic	An approach where the whole is more important than its separate parts.
Hyperbole	Exaggeration for effect.
Image	A picture the writer makes in words, even if it's using one of the other senses besides sight.
Interior	Inside.
Interior Monologue	One person's thinking.
Interpretation	The meaning of something to someone.

Language	Vocabulary that writers use as well as types and variety of sentences.
Mastery	Ability to do something very well.
Mechanics	Punctuation, capitalization, some aspects of grammar.
Monologue	One person speaking.
Narrative	Writing or speaking about people, places, or events.
Organization	How ideas in the piece of writing are ordered—what comes first, middle, and last and how ideas are developed through paragraphs.
Precise	Exact.
Proficient	Ability to do something well.
Relevant	Having meaning related to the topic.
Rubric Features	Categories, or essential elements, of each writing task; listed at the top of each rubric and containing different sets of descriptions to distinguish score point levels.
Scoring Guide	Measurement tool for evaluating writing; a rubric.
Sentence Type	The way a sentence is put together: simple, compound, complex, compound-complex.
Sentence Variety	A mix of sentence types.
"Showing" Writing	Writing that uses details and images to help make a point or create an effect; the opposite of "telling" writing.
Significance	Importance.
Specific	Exact or precise.
Strategies	The bag of tricks a writer uses to put together an effective essay: may include description, dialogue, interior monologue, addressing reader directly, parallelism, and other techniques.
Structure	The way a piece of writing is organized.
Subject-Verb Agreement	Singular subject matching a singular verb; plural matching plural.
Support a Claim	To back up a statement with facts or illustrative anecdotes, examples, and so on.
Syntax	Sentence structure.
"Telling" Writing	Writing that describes and explains without including details or giving examples.
Training Papers	Papers representing a range of scores that beginning scorers use to practice; often used with anchor papers as guides.
Transitions	How the writer moves in words from one part or paragraph of the essay to another.
Underdeveloped	Not elaborated or developed sufficiently to help the reader follow ideas.
Visualize	Get a picture in the mind.
Vivid	Clearly painted—often in words.
Voice	The writer's personality and attitude conveyed through humor, vocabulary, opinions, and strategies such as addressing the reader.
Writing Genres	Writing *types*—varying in purpose, organization, and level of formality.

Identify strengths of the writing. Read through a student paper swiftly, taking note of the writer's overall success at achieving the stated purpose. For example, if the purpose was to describe a childhood passion, do you get a complete and vivid picture of that passion? If the purpose was to persuade you to get rid of vending machines at school, are you convinced? Ask yourself to identify what the writer does well and make a quick mental note of that.

Match the writing to the rubric. As you read, look for a preponderance of evidence in the writing that corresponds to a level on the rubric. Where is the greatest match in the score-point descriptions?

Score the paper. If you've had even minimal experience with holistic scoring, you know that papers can fall within a rather broad range for the same score point. For example, there are high 3's and low 3's. There are solid 4's and weak 4's. In assigning whole-number scores, it's important to remember that each score point can represent a *broad range of writing.*

In addition, you'll almost always come across writing that shows evidence of rubric features across levels. What to do, for example, with a paper that has distinct and expressive voice (corresponding to a 4 descriptor on the rubric), but where the writing shows limited control of conventions and where errors are distracting? Where is there the most evidence? Into which level does *most* of the writing fall? If you can answer this question, if most of the writing demonstrates expressive voice, the ideas are carried by the writer's control of expression, and the errors are easy to ignore because the strengths outshine the mechanical errors, then your score will likely be 3, reflecting aspects of both the 2 and the 4.

Scoring warm-up. Let's try scoring two papers from Lesson 1, "A Personal Oasis."

We've dropped personal biases and reread the rubric. We note that we're going to pay attention to what is noted on the rubric: description, organization, voice, use of language (sentences and vocabulary), and mechanics (spelling and grammar).

We are particularly mindful of the distinctions between score points 2 and 3, since that awareness helps us determine proficiency. Specifically, we note that a *clear description of a place, ideas well organized,* and *sentence variety* with *control of conventions* will place a paper in the 3—*Proficient*—range. Read the rubric and the accompanying paper.

Rubric

Five Features of Descriptive Writing

- Description
- Organization of Ideas
- Writer's Voice
- Language: Sentences and Vocabulary
- Mechanics: Spelling and Grammar

SCORING GUIDE FOR WRITING ABOUT A PLACE

4 • COMMENDABLE

- Description is vivid and well elaborated through a variety of descriptive strategies such as images, anecdotes, and illustrative details that enable the reader to clearly imagine the place.
- Beginning is engaging and description is presented in a clever or unusual way; conclusion ties elements of description together.
- Writing reflects author's thoughts and feelings through commentary, interior monologue, dialogue, description of thoughts or feelings, or by directly addressing the reader.
- Language is lively and expressive; sentences are varied; vocabulary is rich and precise.
- Writing shows mastery of mechanics, though there may be a few errors.

3 • PROFICIENT

- Description is clear and elaborated; the reader has a complete picture of the place, though there may be more "telling" than "showing."
- There is a clear beginning, middle, and conclusion, and writing includes transitions from one part to another.
- Writing reflects author's thoughts and feelings directly or indirectly.
- Language is clear; some sentence variety; vocabulary is general rather than specific.
- Writing shows control of writing conventions; errors do not interfere with meaning.

2 • NEARLY PROFICIENT

- Description is underdeveloped and may not be clear; reader has questions.
- Place is introduced, but writing moves too fast; conclusion may be abrupt or missing.
- Writing may not seem connected to writer through any sense of voice.
- Language is simple; sentence types are mostly the same or simple; vocabulary is limited.
- Writing shows limited control of conventions; errors are distracting.

1 • DEVELOPING

- Description is vague or incomplete; writing may be only a list without elaboration.
- Introduction, middle, or conclusion may be unclear or missing; extremely brief.
- Writing does not show writer's personality or tell why place is meaningful.
- Language may be general and vague, or there may be incomplete or run-on sentences.
- Errors may make it difficult for reader to understand ideas.

Jonny | 9/30/04

My Speacial Place

My special place is my back porch and yard. It is very exciting. I get to expierents wild life in my yard. Many animals come at night and eat our grass and trash. I here cricket and grasshoppers every night. It is very agravating some times. It always hard to get some sleep out on the porch. It is comfortable out on my porch. I love my place. My back yard is so huge a lot of cattle can sleep and maneuver in my back yard.

Another thing is that we can play and have fun there. We can play all types of sports like baseball, basketball, football, soccer, and doge ball. Me and my friends play there a lot. We play for honor, pride, and fun. I have one of the most anormise back yards in town. Many people love it. Its safe, fun, and enjoying. It is very fun for kids to run and exersise during the games.

> The porch is also part of the back yard. It has tile flores and has a table with chairs. The chairs are very comfortable. They are as soft as a pupies furr. It has stairs that lead to the back yard. The porch has all sorts of things balls, equitment, and a grill for yummie delights. From the porch I could see down the street where the pleses lived.
>
> The porch and the Back yard were very asome. And they still are asome. I think the porch and my backyard is the place were my kids can play and be free. That is when I grow up and get married to my dream girl. It is a dream place to imagine.
>
> This was imortant because I wanted to tell about my speacial place. The house that I live in now is were my porch is and backyard is. I hope I can stay there all my life. I love my special place.

In reading "My Special Place," we notice that the author immediately identifies his personal oasis and begins elaboration. The writer is able to identify the unique and personally meaningful aspects of his special place. Although we note that the writer successfully conveys that the place is special, and although we note many specific details, the writing is linear (list-like) and the sentences are the same: almost uniformly simple sentences. As readers, we have questions about the relative importance of the backyard, of the porch, of the activities, and of the flora and fauna that exist. This piece corresponds directly to the features outlined for score point 2, *Nearly Proficient.* Conventions are problematic and errors are distracting. However, we can say that the writer is clearly on his way toward proficiency. The raw material is present.

Let's look at a second paper, "A Place."

"A Place"

	9/30/04
	A Place Shannon

     Have you ever had a special place that you loved so much that every time you blinked or every time you felt your heart rate you thought of that special place. This place of yours; Does it make you happy, sad, or does it give you energy?

     My favorite place to go is not in public. It is not where other people go. It is not a place with invitations like parties. My favorite place is my favorite place and my favorite place only. It is not any ones favorite place but mine. It may seem strange but my favorite place is in my mind.

     My mind is unique. My mind is unique because nobody can think like me. Only I can think like that. My mind is almost like a mall because of all the entries there is. It is a nice little thinking place, a quotes zone, a come up fast thinking shop, and I even made room for a place where I go to talk to girls on the phone.

     I think out of all the little places in my mind would have to be the place where I go to talk on the phone to girls. I think the reason it is my favorite is because that is

what I do best. That is where I say what I
say and is always at the right time. I love to
hang out there because there is so much to
do. I have turned my mind into a real man's
mind. I have so many catagories and in every
catagorie I have a certain time to say it and
if I miss the time the comment or question
gets deleted from my mind for ever.

First, the ideas are original, and the approach is fresh. The writer is assertive (if slightly repetitive), and the voice is distinctive and convincing. The use of language is clear, and as we read, we're beginning to place this in the high range, 3 or 4. However, as we continue reading, we notice that the vocabulary is more general than specific and that the sentences are mostly of the same structure. It's not clear that this is intentional—a by-product of sentence control for purposes of rhythmic effect. In fact, we suspect that this indicates the writer's limited repertoire. As we proceed with a swift read, we see that although the essay began with a compelling introduction and developed well, there is no conclusion. This lack of an ending shifts our potential score of 4 directly to a 3. With a little coaching (and attention to the importance of varied sentence types and strategies and fitting conclusions), this writer will be functioning at a 4 level soon.

TEACHING STUDENTS TO SCORE

If you teach at a small school (perhaps a combined grade-level class), or if your school (or grade level) is not one where you could collaborate for a community writing assessment, you're on your own for the scoring. Many teachers in that position have found it effective to teach their students to score. You can administer the prewriting activities, have students write their essays, and set aside a certain day in which to teach the rubric and have students score them. We recommend a day or two as hiatus between the writing of the essays and the reading of them; such minor distance allows students to take a fresh look at the writing, and looking afresh is essential in any holistic scoring.

Let's call the day after that hiatus Day One.

Day One is training day. Pass around a rubric to each student. Now, train the students, score point by score point. Some teachers like to start at the top of the scoring guide and work down, others from the bottom up. Talk about the terms in the scoring guide and refer to the "Rubric Tip Sheet." Give examples as often as possible. This mini-training and the discussion that ensues will take at least half a normal period—sometimes an entire period. (Use one or more student exemplars. Do you have examples from classes of previous years? Great! Student examples are powerful: use them!)

Day Two is scoring day. Put a piece of blue masking tape (the removable type) over the name of each student on each paper. Shuffle the papers. Pass them around, one per student, asking students to let you know if they get their own papers. Have students quietly read this first essay. During *this* reading, be interruptive: point out rubric characteristics, exhorting students to look for those characteristics, helping again to interpret them. Tell students you won't be interrupting so much on others, but *do* be intrusive on this first one, saying things like, "Does the essay have a clear beginning, middle, and end? How are the ideas organized? Are they easy to follow? Where on the rubric does the organization of the writing you're scoring fall?"

While the students are reading, and between your interruptions, circulate in the classroom, tearing off a few pieces of blue tape and sticking them on the edge of each desk. Have each student score this first paper on the 1–4 scale, initialing the score and putting a scrap of blue tape over the score and initials. As the students finish that, they should switch papers with someone. You act as go-between, helping students make connections with others who are finished.

We think it's a good idea to have three students score each paper according to this method. The third student averages the three and writes an overall score. (If you're using our "Writing Sample" template from Appendix D, that overall average goes in the square on the last page.) Collect the papers. Discuss the process, how it went, and what students can report they learned.

Now, read the papers yourself, scoring each conspicuously so that each student knows the difference between students' averages and yours. (You'll be surprised at how often their scores and yours are consonant.)

What's positive about this method? It's intimate: students are reading *their* classmates' essays, recognizing handwriting, perhaps familiar with a few phrases certain students often use, and the family feeling, in a classroom where respect is paramount, can be strong. What doesn't work about it? Unless example papers are available, the process of feeling confident about what constitutes a particular score point is missing, and students' scores drift. And since you as teacher have only *these* papers to discuss, you *can* point out strong characteristics of essays, but *can't,* really, publicly point out their flaws.

Finally, you're the only adult reading them, and you may be off on a few, missing the benefit of a second or third adult reading. Nonetheless, this process is better, we think, than simply reading the papers solo and handing them back to students scored only by you. In Chapter Seven we describe two methods when students (re)score papers after a large-scale assessment.

Using the Prompts in Larger-Scale Writing Assessments

Larger-scale writing assessments are extremely valuable and are common practice in many school districts. Community scoring events can empower faculties by giving teachers local control over writing assessments and providing immediate results, and they can be used to directly improve instruction. They can include teachers of subjects other than English in the conversation about what constitutes good writing and how to teach it, and include students at all levels—including English learners and Special Education—in the dynamic process of writing improvement. In effect, the value of having students complete an on-demand writing assessment increases as the community scoring and analysis of the writing grows.

At a community scoring, each piece of student writing gets two objective reads (and more if the first two readers are more than one point apart). All scorers are trained to apply a whole number from the assignment-specific rubric in consistent ways to each piece of student writing. Having participated in a holistic scoring process at an earlier time does not constitute having been trained for *this* scoring, though it does familiarize people with the process.

Group or schoolwide writing assessments require organization and leadership to be successful. When done right, the scoring process (which deepens teachers' understanding of writing) and product (final scores and accompanying analyses) have the power to dramatically enhance instruction that improves student writing. The process can also unify a faculty by developing common writing goals and a shared vocabulary about writing, and it supports teacher professional development by focusing on student work.

The prompts in this book can be used for broader grade-level or schoolwide writing assessments just as effectively as for single classroom use. We've worked with many schools that schedule one, two, or three schoolwide writing assessments over the course of a school year. In multi-class or multi-grade assessments, all students write to the same prompt (and are thus evaluated with the same scoring guide), which teachers have selected together. Sometimes the writing occurs in a class other than English to demonstrate to students that writing (and thus thinking) is done in all classes. Teachers administer the assessment during the same window and submit student papers to a leadership team. This team organizes the scoring and resulting reports and analyses.

This is a terrifically powerful process. Once instituted and institutionalized year to year, it can change your school to one wherein writing is central to its culture.

PLANNING COMMUNITY ASSESSMENT AND SCORING EVENTS

The assessment and scoring guidelines provided here assume that your scoring will be for more than a single class. No matter how large or small the scoring, certain arrangements need to be made so the process is valid and reliable (and fun). Though the procedure may seem long at first, the steps become much easier as community scoring events become familiar. To begin, the following sections provide some global guidelines.

Selection of Facilitator and Leadership Team

The exercise needs one person (teacher, administrator, counselor, for example) who facilitates the assessment planning and scoring process. This person should be well-organized, committed to writing growth, good at delegating, and willing and able to serve as general (cheer)leader for both the training session and the formal scoring.

It also needs several other people to form a small leadership team. These might be teachers who've had experience in holistic scoring, or would like to acquire experience. They will choose anchor and training papers and provide general assistance during the scoring process. If you're staging a whole faculty scoring, these might be the teachers most experienced at teaching and evaluating writing. In addition to planning and scheduling a scoring event and arranging the room, it's great if the leadership team takes responsibility for providing refreshments and supplies. Refreshments introduce a note of grace to the project, and everyone's commitment and attention seems to improve. Scorers will need pencils, highlighters (for marking rubrics), blank paper (for taking notes), and Post-it® notes for tagging papers they want to refer to a counselor or to copy for instructional purposes.

Scheduling Considerations

Scheduling of the writing assessments is an important step in assuring success. Teachers need lots of lead time to build the assessment and scoring into their plans. It's best to decide on dates for community scoring events early in the school year. You'll need to consider blocking out time periods for scoring in the following ways.

If you are doing a grade-level or whole-school writing and scoring, give teachers the "window" of a full week to administer the total writing lesson. Teachers submit student papers (no prewriting materials, just student essays appropriately identified) to a central location on the last day of the testing week. In this way, teachers have flexibility to determine when they implement the lesson and when students actually write. Aside from designating dates by which the tests should be completed, schedulers need to plan time for the following activities for scorers:

- *Selection of anchor and training papers:* The leadership team selects these for use in the scoring. This takes anywhere from one to two hours depending on how much people want to talk about each paper.

- *Training session:* The facilitator leads this at the general scoring session. The training session introduces scorers to the prompt and the rubric and gives important practice in scoring sample papers. This can take from one to two hours. We've found that when we invest time to do a thorough training, the scoring is much more reliable and scorers can proceed with scoring swiftly and confidently.

- *The scoring:* The facilitator guides this session, managing the papers as they are scored once, then twice, and intervening during the process to announce breaks, to ask participants to share helpful scoring tips, to clear up any confusion, and to keep the momentum swift.

- *Recording final scores:* This is done by the facilitator or leadership team. Final scores are entered on class lists, and schoolwide and individual class averages are calculated. This step is important to plan for (and allot time for), as results returned swiftly to students and teachers have the best chance of being folded back into instruction. We recommend that the leadership team take no longer than one week to compile results of the community writing assessment. Beyond two weeks, the thread can be lost, and the process becomes less meaningful to students.

A community training and scoring event can be scheduled a couple of different ways. The preferred method is to complete the entire process in all or most of a school day. But if a full day is not available, we've scheduled training and scoring sessions after school over a week or two. Allow enough time in the scoring for discussions of papers difficult to score and for scorers to take breaks as they read. How long does it take to read all the papers twice? Plan for roughly ten-minute reads, six papers an hour, for novice scorers and double the number of papers in that same time for experienced scorers. Remembering that each paper is read twice, the following formula should help you plan enough time for scoring:

$$\text{Number of Papers} \times 15 \text{ Minutes (Two Reads)} +$$
$$\text{Enough Time for Breaks and Comments} =$$
$$\text{Time You'll Need to Complete a Large-Scale Scoring}$$

(*Note:* The facilitator will want to remind scorers once or twice during the session that they're not "correcting" papers but swiftly reading them to evaluate their holistic strengths.)

MAKING TIME FOR A COMMUNITY SCORING

How to make time for scorers to participate in a community scoring in a crowded school schedule? For teachers participating in or coordinating a scoring on top of their full-time teaching responsibilities, it's appropriate (and necessary) to grant them release time or a professional stipend, or both. For the training and scoring session, some schools use professional development days; others schedule scoring on several afternoons after school. (Of course, we assume that teachers asked to come in after school are *paid* for their time. There's nothing like an unpaid scoring session to completely undermine future staff support for schoolwide or grade-level scoring.)

A third method is that in which some schools arrange for substitutes to cover classes while shifts of regular teachers cycle through the scoring during the day: a morning shift and an afternoon shift. (This method assumes that the training for the holistic scoring has occurred either the day before or with *all parties involved* on the morning of the scoring.)

WHO CAN PARTICIPATE IN A COMMUNITY SCORING?

It's presumed that the classroom teachers of students whose papers are being evaluated would participate. In addition to these teachers (for in scorings, many hands and minds do make lighter work), it's often appropriate and possible to include other members of the school community: administrators, counselors, teacher aides, resource teachers, tech teachers, and even parent volunteers. After students are trained in applying holistic rubrics, they, too, can be scorers. The important point is to gather members of the school community who can be objective, and who can accurately peg student essays to the rubric.

SELECTION OF ANCHOR AND TRAINING PAPERS

For a scoring event to be reliable, scorers must be anchored in a solid understanding of what the terms of the rubric mean and how those terms translate to student writing. Though you can use scored papers from another assessment, the best anchor papers are those that come directly from the assessment being scored. If this is not possible, you can use appropriate exemplars included in Appendix A.

The anchor packet is a set of four student papers (prescored and labeled) that provide examples of writing corresponding to each score point on the rubric. The papers are labeled as follows: *Fall/Winter/Spring [Year] Writing Assessment: ANCHOR 4, Fall/Winter/Spring [Year] Writing Assessment: ANCHOR 3, Fall/Winter/Spring [Year] Writing Assessment: ANCHOR 2, Fall/Winter/Spring [Year] Writing Assessment: ANCHOR 1.* These anchor papers are used to translate the language of the rubric (for teachers or later, students) and make the holistic scoring process concrete. (It's also useful to refer to these in subsequent assessments to make sure your standards haven't shifted.)

Prior to a scoring event, the leadership team meets to select four student essays to be included in the anchor packet. In creating this packet, it can be helpful to assemble a separate training packet at the same time. The training packet includes four additional student papers (also representing each of the rubric score point levels) and is used for giving the scorers practice in evaluating the essays. Anchor and training papers are pulled from the entire collection of student writing, and leadership team members take note of issues particular to the task (that is, students took a variety of approaches to the prompt, certain students compressed the activity into one day, several groups word-processed their essays in the lab, and so on) to forewarn scorers about what they may notice and pave the way for a smooth scoring.

Although the training papers are already scored by the leadership team, they're left *unlabeled,* and presented to the scorers in random order. (We explain the process for training scorers later in the chapter.) After anchor and training papers are selected, copied, labeled, and duplicated for all scorers, the papers that haven't been scored need to be randomized into stacks. We call these stacks *batches,* and we've found that fifteen to twenty papers in a batch works best. Generally, all members of the leadership team score all the anchor and training papers.

We begin by reading a handful of papers from a variety of classes. When twenty to thirty papers have been read and scored by everyone, we stop, talk about what we're finding, and look for papers for which everyone has agreed on the same score. These generally are solid examples of the different score point levels. We talk about features of the rubric that help us with a holistic evaluation; we compare our impressions of the student writing—where there are strengths and weaknesses. In this way we come to agreement about best representatives of each score point.

Sometimes we have to look for papers in the low and high ends to complete the anchor or training packets. The process is valuable: it functions as a training for the leadership team. The anchor papers, training papers, and all additional papers that have been scored in the process of assembling the packets need not be scored again. Final scores are recorded and these are tucked away in the "Scored" pile.

To summarize, the following ten steps help you assure a smooth process in *preparing for a community scoring:*

1. *Review the prompt.* Discuss subtleties or the various approaches students took. Talk about students' responses to the prompt: Did they like it? Have lots to write? Feel prepared?

2. *Reread the rubric.* Clarify terms. Refer to the "Rubric Tip Sheet" if necessary. Discuss distinctions in levels.

3. *Agree on a method for scoring and keeping scores anonymous.* We use different colors of Post-it® notes (one color for each Leadership Team member) and have each person record a score on the sticky side. This way we know who has scored the paper, we can monitor which scorers may be evaluating too severely or too liberally, and we can adjust this through discussion. The Post-it® notes are quick and easy for moving from paper to paper.

4. *Begin reading and scoring.* Pull a random selection of papers from the entire collection of student writing and work with these.

5. *Pause and talk about the papers and the scores.* Are there lots of 3's, 2's? Is it easy to find a correspondence between the writing and the rubric levels? What helpful tips do people have to share?

6. *Proceed assembling anchor and training packets.* Continue scoring with an eye to filling out a complete packet for anchoring and for training. Look for the best examples of each score point. Because student writing can reflect high and low ends within a single

score point, scorers should look for writing that falls right smack in the middle of the score point range. (It may sometimes be difficult to find student examples corresponding to the highest and lowest ends of the rubric. If so, assemble an incomplete anchor packet. Not finding examples at the low end of the rubric is good news!) In addition, it's great if you can find anchor and training examples that are legible and photocopy well. Difficult-to-read or illegibly photocopied examples are frustrating for all readers, teachers and students alike. It's also useful to select anchor papers that are fun to read and elevate the morale of the scorers.

7. *Assemble and label the anchor packet and the training packet.* Organize the anchor packet from highest to lowest score, organize the training packet randomly, and prepare these for duplicating. Make sure you note the scores of the training packet so you can refer to them later. Record final scores of all the other papers that were read and scored (but not selected for a packet) and put them aside.

8. *Duplicate the prompt, rubric, and anchor and training packets.* You will need copies for each scorer participating in the scoring session.

9. *Randomize the remaining student papers and organize them into batches of fifteen to twenty.* The papers have been labeled (by students) to maintain anonymity, but they're still organized by class, so mix them up. If you're doing a multi-grade assessment, all the papers are treated similarly, measured against the same rubric. Randomizing the papers is an additional way of guaranteeing objectivity during the scoring process.

10. *Choose a facilitator to guide the scoring.* Arrange for the scoring location and for refreshments.

STAGING THE COMMUNITY SCORING

Now it's time to train the scorers themselves—that cadre of willing readers. This training can be brief, but it *must* take place in order to establish common standards. The training is also a productive tool for deepening the understanding of writing and writing instruction for novice or non-English subject teachers; it's most effective when it takes place the actual day of the scoring, but if the scoring falls on more than one day (after school, for example), we have managed quite well training one afternoon and scoring another. The facilitator will want to determine training time based on the number of new scorers. The larger the number of veteran scorers, obviously, the more swiftly you can move through the training. We believe that two hours for training is a maximum time allotment—usually a much shorter time suffices.

The facilitator has an important role in leading a scoring session: to balance the support and encouragement scorers need while maintaining strict adherence to the evaluation standards established in the rubric and anchor papers. Holistic scoring takes practice and reassurance. A facilitator who can be positive and lighthearted and at the same time focused on completing the scoring accurately and efficiently is a great asset. Before launching the training (and subsequent scoring), the facilitator should make sure that copies of the rubric, the anchor packet, and the training packet have been distributed.

Here's our "lucky-thirteen-step program" for staging a scoring session:

1. Welcome scorers and review the prompt. Participants should read (or reread) the prompt; not all of them will have seen it before, and all can use the refresher.

2. Introduce scorers to the use of holistic rubrics. Distribute the "Rubric Tip Sheet" if that's helpful. Refer to our rationale for holistic evaluation in Chapter Five. Remember that using a rubric and applying it holistically may be new for your group of scorers. They'll need (and deserve) the rationale and some practice with support and encouragement.

3. Read the rubric and the anchor papers, one score point level at a time. The facilitator (half-facilitator and half-cheerleader, really) asks scorers to look for correspondences between the rubric features and the student writing. It's great, if there's time, to do this process orally, welcoming teacher comments along the way. Point out that scores should be based on

- Strengths (rather than weaknesses) of the writing.

- *Only* features identified in the rubric (therefore, not handwriting, length of paper or number of paragraphs, or particular teachers' pet peeves not in the rubric).

- A match between student writing and features described on the rubric. Sometimes students are strong in one or two areas (say, organization of ideas and elaboration of ideas, and not in spelling or punctuation). Scorers look for the features that are *most present* in the student writing. This is called a "preponderance of evidence" in the student writing that corresponds to the rubric.

4. Read and score papers in the training packet. This is your way of determining how successful the training was. Ask scorers to hold themselves accountable to the rubric and explain that they will be asked to share their scores. When scoring is completed, the facilitator should do a quick public (and visual) assessment of the scores. When we're facilitating, we do this by sketching a grid like the one on page 44 on a chart at the front of the room (or on a chalkboard), with the left-hand column listing the titles of each paper in the order they appear in the training packet. Across the top of the grid we jot the score points. Then we move through each of the training papers, asking scorers to raise their hands when we call out the score they gave that paper. We record the number of scores for each score point and quickly determine the degree of agreement among scorers.

5. Present the scores the Leadership Team determined by circling the score point box on the grid.

6. Invite scorers who agreed with the Leadership Team to talk about why they assigned the scores they did. Remind them to use language from the rubric, but don't shut them down if they elaborate or wax enthusiastic.

7. Invite scorers who disagreed with the Leadership Team to talk about why they assigned the scores they did. Either the facilitator or another scorer can point out rubric features in the writing to persuade this person to agree with the score. After converting the outlying scorers (or adjusting the Leadership Team's scores slightly) you're ready to proceed with scoring. If there's wide disagreement (two-point differences, for example) we extend the discussion and point out the correspondences between the writing and the rubric.

```
┌─────────────────────────────────────────────────────────────────────┐
│                         Training Packet Grid                          │
│  ───────────────────────────────────────────────────────────────────│
│  In each box, the facilitator writes the number of scorers who indi- │
│  cate they assigned the corresponding score.                          │
│                                                                       │
│  ┌──────────────────────────┬──────┬──────┬──────┬──────┐            │
│  │ Training Paper Titles     │  4   │  3   │  2   │  1   │            │
│  ├──────────────────────────┼──────┼──────┼──────┼──────┤            │
│  │ (Title of Student Paper)  │      │      │      │      │            │
│  ├──────────────────────────┼──────┼──────┼──────┼──────┤            │
│  │ (Title of Student Paper)  │      │      │      │      │            │
│  ├──────────────────────────┼──────┼──────┼──────┼──────┤            │
│  │ (Title of Student Paper)  │      │      │      │      │            │
│  ├──────────────────────────┼──────┼──────┼──────┼──────┤            │
│  │ (Title of Student Paper)  │      │      │      │      │            │
│  └──────────────────────────┴──────┴──────┴──────┴──────┘            │
└─────────────────────────────────────────────────────────────────────┘
```

Feel free to move on if the clear majority of scorers is agreeing with the scores the Leadership Team gave to each of the training papers. If there are a few outlying scores on the grid (either higher or lower), these scorers tend to calibrate themselves, noting that they were consistently higher or lower than the rest of the group, and they adjust their scoring appropriately.

Scorers keep their (often annotated) anchor and training papers to refer to as scoring proceeds. Sometimes these concrete representations of the rubric score points help scorers stay consistent over many reads. After the scoring session, we encourage scorers to keep training materials to use for instruction.

8. Explain how participants are to record their scores. How are scores recorded? We know of three effective methods to record (and then conceal) scores, as shown in the figure on page 45.

9. Proceed with first reads. When the facilitator is confident that scorers are ready to proceed with confidence and accuracy, begin scoring papers. During this period of first reads, each paper is read and scored. Participants take a batch of papers (one of those previously randomized stacks), then read and record scores (according to the selected method) for each one. Scorers should be encouraged to develop a swift momentum that facilitates holistic evaluation. Once again, scorers should look for the features that resonate, that call out to the scorer. The scorer then links these features (it gets quicker and quicker) and records a score.

Methods of Recording Scores

Method 1: The first method is to have students write on a preprinted form—like the one included in Appendix D—with a box for student information and three circles at the top of the first page. The circle on the left is for the first score, the middle circle is for the second, and the circle on the right is for the final score, which is the average of scores 1 and 2. Teachers write their initials outside the circles to avoid reading the same papers twice.

Method 2: The second method is to record scores on different-colored Post-it® notes or in different-colored ink. Scorers write on the back side (sticky side) of the Post-it® note to conceal their scores. Final scores are recorded on the front of the essay.

Method 3: The third method has scorers write on batch sheets (see Appendix E), which prevents writing anything on student papers. This method requires the extra step of recording student ID codes or numbers on the batch sheets and then keeping the papers in the exact same order for both readings. This can be cumbersome, time-consuming, and vulnerable to mistakes, but it often results in very speedy scoring. Note that readers initial and fold under the column they've used to obscure their scores for the next reader.

In a few cases, a scorer may want to resist scoring a paper. The facilitator should alert scorers to withhold scores in the following cases:

- The scorer recognizes the student's handwriting and doesn't feel able to be objective.
- Something that the writer expresses is offensive to the scorer and it is not possible to score objectively.
- Something deeply personal and troubling has appeared in the writing; a counselor's guidance is called for, and scoring such a paper is not appropriate.
- The paper is illegible.
- The student writes on a topic completely outside the prompt.

What to do with these? In the first two cases, the scorer simply passes the paper on to another scorer. In the case of the "counselor needed" paper, some schools collect these in a box or folder labeled "Referred to a Counselor," and the facilitator makes sure counselors see *copies* of those papers, in order to provide appropriate follow-up with students, which then get scored like other papers. In the case of illegibility or off-topic responses, we leave this to the decision of the classroom teacher; some allow students to do a rewrite while others let the papers go unscored and use this as an opportunity to emphasize the importance of writing legibly or reading the prompt carefully.

10. Proceed with second reads. That is, after papers are read once, they get read a second time by someone else. The second reader proceeds swiftly (by the second read, most scorers are moving apace), and records a second score.

11. Take brief and frequent breaks. The facilitator can invite scorers to share effective strategies for landing on the right score, ask participants to share observations about trends in student writing and share amusing quotes from student writing. Scorers can note words or expressions from student writing, read these aloud during breaks, or record them on the board. They showcase student ingenuity and give people a chance to laugh.

12. After first and second reads are completed, record final scores. These are the average of the first two scores. If there is time during the scoring session, the second reader averages and records the final score. If time is running short, we usually ask scorers to read and not take time to average and record. The facilitator or Leadership Team can do this later.

13. Finally, the papers need to be unbatched and resegregated into various teachers' classes. In a large school, handling, say, a thousand papers, this task can be daunting and time-consuming. But we've found that with a little willing student labor, it can be completed efficiently and can help grow a school's writing culture. How? Mark in felt pen pieces of paper with each teacher's name. If someone teaches multiple classes, do a separate paper for each. Tape those papers on classroom desks, distribute papers to one class, and have students place papers in their proper category—"Martinez, 1st period" and so on. Voilà! In just a few hectic minutes the papers are where they need to be.

Learning from the Assessment Process

You've got your papers back and in a stack, either from the schoolwide or gradewide or class scoring. For an assessment to be worth the time it takes to administer and evaluate, it should yield results that you can use to improve student writing. So now what can you do with them before handing them back and having students put them in their portfolios? There are many ways to use both the papers and their results. But first, if you completed a community scoring, you'll want to read the papers over. A word about the role of the teacher as score arbiter. *Mistakes are made,* for holistic scoring is difficult and (sometimes) goes on for a long time. Scorers get tired and can lose their ability to score accurately.

Look at the essays. Did a student who wrote an edgy, risk-taking essay get a low score from some rather conservative teachers, or from teachers who may not be teachers of writing and are strict constructionists when it comes to the anchors? Did a student's horrible handwriting obviously influence the scorers' judgment? You may want to not *change* the score, for the integrity of the process is compromised by that, but you may want to either write a personal *comment* on the paper "Miguel, I disagree with this score. I would have scored it a 3." or write something like "Jones's (your name) Score: 4." (And *do* say, more than once, "By the way, if any of you have any question or disagreement *at all* with the score you received, come and talk with me! We'll look at it again.")

WHAT ABOUT GRADES?

The sequence we honor and the one we've described throughout this book is *holistic* and *process-oriented.* With that in mind, we believe a teacher must resist the temptation to grade each paper. Yes, each paper *does* represent a student's effort—in most cases intensive effort, in some cases not. And each effort is *data,* but ought not to receive a letter grade.

Why? Because the goal is gradually to improve each individual student's writing. And each student is *individually* somewhere on the continuum that runs from beginning writer to sophisticated writer. And every writer can improve. So assigning a letter grade to an essay in this process can indeed be counterproductive.

Furthermore, grades are subjective, relying on a host of variables individual teachers consider. Scores reflecting rubric features reduce the subjectivity of a grading system. Should Mario, for example, who received a score of 2, get a "C" on his paper, even though he tried ferociously hard and broke new ground for himself in length? Should Maria, who easily scored a 4 but used her tried-and-true rhetorical devices—the same she's been using for two years, almost a formula for her now—receive an "A" because of that high score? You can see the inherent contradictions—and contraindications—of assigning letter grades.

Better, perhaps, to structure the process as a kind of class participation—it's simply expected as a normal part of the overall grade. It exists, and one gets plenty of credit for it— that *plenty* spelled out specifically, if you need to, according to your credit system—for participating fully. (And what if a student *doesn't* participate fully—disrupts or slouches or scribbles three lines only when it's essay time? There's no easy answer to that. You know your students. Student A might do that because his skills are so profoundly low that the entire process is beyond him, and your state or city Special Education policy will not allow him the help he needs. Student B might have the skills and be a professional obstructionist; in his case, a firm urging from you—or a suggestion he leave the class while the hard workers are doing their jobs—might get him going.)

It's important that students *themselves* know that they're engaged in process here: that their writing won't jump from a 1 to a 4 overnight, that achieving excellence in writing is a process of accretion, layering, and that each week or month provides the opportunity to add another layer of knowledge or another strategy to their inventory of skills. Reinforcing this concept of *process,* then, is essential in the creation and nurturing of a community of writers. So we do recommend a grade for participating (perhaps a self-assessment) as students monitor their progress as writers measured longitudinally by keeping a record of their rubric scores.

TAKING A CLOSER LOOK AT RESULTS

So you've got your papers. Take a look at them. How do they average? Are they 1's and 2's, primarily? Or 3's and 4's? A wild mix? Who are your students? Are they native speakers? Honors students? English language learners? Special Education? Your knowledge of your class, its levels, and its potential will help tailor your instructional responses to this assessment. We recommend that you consider disaggregating the results by the student categories listed here or by others that are significant for you. A score-point distribution chart is easy to complete and helpful in assisting you to see patterns in your students' writing. The chart is useful in studying overall class performance, and it helps you monitor growth over time when applied to several assessments. Two examples of results charts are shown here: an overall class score point distribution and a score point distribution by gender. Use these and adapt them to help you monitor results of additional subgroups.

Score Point Distribution

Scores, Percentages and Mean Score for Lesson: _____

Total Number of Students _____   Number of Scored Papers _____

1. Tally the number of papers for each score point.

	4	3.5	3	2.5	2	1.5	1
All Students							

2. Now calculate percentages at each score point. To do this, multiply the number of papers at each score point by 100, then divide this sum by the total number of scored papers.

For example, if 8 student papers got a score of 3, and the total number of scored papers is 25, the calculation looks like this:

$$8 \times 100/25 = 32$$

That is, 32 percent of the scored papers received a 3. Now complete percentage calculations for each score point.

3. Percentages at each score point:

	4	3.5	3	2.5	2	1.5	1
All Students							

4. What percentage of papers were scored *Commendable* (4)? _____

5. What percentage of papers were scored *Proficient* (3)? _____

6. What percentage of papers were scored *Nearly Proficient* (2)? _____

7. What is the class mean score? _____   (Calculate this by multiplying the number of students at each score point by that score point. Add these sums, then divide by the total number of scored papers.)

Score Point Distribution by Gender

Gender Results for Lesson: _____

Total Number of Students _____

Number of Girls _____   Number of Boys _____

1. To complete a gender analysis of your class results, tally the number of papers for each score point for girls and boys.

	4	3.5	3	2.5	2	1.5	1
Girls							
Boys							

2. Now calculate gender percentages at each score point. To do this, multiply the number of papers at each score point by 100, then divide this sum by the total number of scored papers.

   For example, if 8 student papers got a score of 3, and the total number of scored papers is 25, the calculation looks like this:

$$8 \times 100/25 = 32$$

That is, 32 percent of the scored papers received a 3. Now complete percentage calculations for each score point.

	4	3.5	3	2.5	2	1.5	1
Girls							
Boys							

3. What percentage of papers by girls were scored *Commendable* (4)? _____ boys? _____

4. What percentage of papers by girls were scored *Proficient* (3)? _____ boys? _____

5. What percentage of papers by girls were scored *Nearly Proficient* (2)? _____ boys? _____

6. What is the mean score for papers by girls? _____ boys? _____ (Calculate this by multiplying the number of students at each score point by that score point. Add these sums, then divide by the total number of scored papers.)

If your students scored primarily in the low range, you've got your work cut out for you, but that work need not be overwhelming. If they're primarily in the high range, your work, too, is cut out, but of a slightly smoother cloth. By looking over the results as they are displayed by score point and by gender or other subgroupings, you can focus follow-up instruction on individual or small groups of students. Depending on where most students scored, you'll want to help students deepen their understanding of, first, what constitutes an essay: its component parts; its expected length; and the concept of beginning, middle, and end; and help them develop substance and find their voice. You'll also want to emphasize skills such as choice of language, sentence variation, rhetorical strategies, and logic, helping them distinguish mere competency from compelling control—all in the context of learning to write more and better under time constraints. Teachers whose classes vary wildly have the most difficult job: threading the wavering needle of instruction high and low. And if that same teacher has a class size that is high, one that virtually obviates the possibility of one-on-one instruction, the task is difficult indeed.

Further complicating the matter is the fact that writing instruction is so much a product of individual tastes, habits, and teaching styles. So our intent in this chapter is not prescriptive—no nostrum here as to how to create terrific writers instantly. Many books have been written toward the idea of creating skilled writers, and within the scope of this book we cannot do it. However, we do believe that some strategies are effective for use in many classes. We'll lay out a few in the remainder of this chapter.

TRAINING STUDENTS TO (RE)SCORE THE WRITING

As we've said in Chapter Five, having students score essays in the classroom can be both a terrific instructional tool and lots of fun. Scorings are possible wherein your class members serve as the only scorers (described on page 35). Student scoring is also possible wherein a rather formal, quiet, "traditional" process is followed after a schoolwide assessment has occurred, with two students reading each paper, each giving scores. An additional and exciting "read-around scoring" can be used, wherein many students read, score, and make quick comments on many papers after the schoolwide assessment. We'll describe the latter two methods here, discuss how to manage them, and share our opinion of their strengths and weaknesses. (In all methods, we recommend using painter's masking tape—the light-duty blue kind that comes off easily—to keep the papers anonymous. You tape over student names with it, and have the students use little pieces of it to tape over their scores.)

Students (Re)Score: Method 1

The first method takes essays already scored by adults—whether in a schoolwide scoring or a grade-level scoring—and has students take a second look. Here's how to do it. Adults have scored the papers and returned your classes' papers to you. Pass out the anchor packets that were used in the community scoring. (The great aspect of this scoring is that you have a packet of anchors from which to teach!) Pass out one rubric to each student. Go over the anchors one by one and ask students to point out how salient features correspond to descriptors in the rubric. (There's plenty to talk about, but try not to make the session a lecture: at a minimum, ask students yes-no questions; the nature of their responses can help you know whether or not they're getting the training.) Refer to the "Rubric Tip Sheet" if necessary. This process usually takes one class period.

When the next class begins, pass out the anchor papers and the rubric and proceed with a quick review. Then tell students that they'll be scoring papers, and ask them if they have any questions regarding the process or regarding characteristics of various score points. Clarify any confusion, then pass out one paper per student. What papers? We've found it best to pass out papers from a different class—perhaps your own second or third class. There's less interference of recognition there, and students can focus more easily on the scoring than the writer. Designate a place for students to enter their scores, with their initials beside each score.

At the next class, have each student read and score one paper, put blue tape over their score (you've stuck three small pieces of tape to the edge of each student's desk before class began), then find another to read. You can time the reads and have students read and then pass the paper on to another designated student—next to, behind, in front of—or you can act as matchmaker and move around the classroom passing off first reads to second readers. The second student reads, scores, then draws a separate box or circle on the paper and averages the two scores in it. If there's a discrepancy of more than one point, have the second reader tape over both scores and pass the paper on to a third reader. After scoring, the third reader takes the highest two scores and averages them for the final score.

Students (Re)Score: Method 2

This one's fun. It incorporates Method 1, but many more students read many more papers, commenting in writing on each one. Here's how to do it.

As with Method 1, pass out the anchor packets. (If there's limited access to photocopy machines or paper, two students can share one packet, or you can put each anchor example up on the overhead projector.) Pass out one scoring guide to each student. Go over the anchor papers one by one, pointing out characteristics of each paper and how each reflects descriptors on the rubric. Depending upon the class, this could occur in half a period, but more likely it'll take an entire period. Have at least one packet of papers ready with the blue masking tape already over students' names and previously determined scores. Have a student put ten or so scraps of blue tape on the edge of each desk.

We've found it effective to read a paper or two orally, asking students as a class to think about what score they might give it, pointing out characteristics ("Did anyone notice the smooth transition this student made? Listen to this again: 'However, though we might think this is true, it's not true at all.' A nice shift, no?") and coming to either an agreement or an agreement-to-disagree on the ultimate score.

Now pass out student papers. Again, it's powerful if the papers can be from another class, so that they're less recognizable, but if that's not possible, the process still works well. Here, though, is where the reading differs from Method 1. Each student is to do a few things:

- Give each paper a careful reading.
- Score each paper (scores can be written in the margins).

- Initial the score.

- Put a piece of tape over the score.

- Write a single comment somewhere on the paper—the comment relating either to something specific ("cool image!") or to the essay in general ("lots of good descriptive writing, but I found the logic hard to follow, and things kinda fell apart in the end").

- Find another paper to score, the teacher functioning again as paper shuffler, getting as many papers read as possible.

By the end of the period, assuming that at least a full period is used for the reading, students have read many essays, placing on them many scores and plenty of peer comments. (A quick note on those peer comments: Some classes will need reminding of the power of positive or at least positively framed comments; no put-downs allowed. Teachers should circulate, making sure that no insulting comments are made, and, before handing papers back to their owners, read them so that any nasty comments that do appear can be crossed out or erased.)

The last reader does not average the scores—there are too many—and simply and slowly removes each piece of blue tape except the piece of tape obscuring the student writer's name, which the teacher later removes. What results in this method is energizing: there's an air of excitement in the room, students receive their papers back with many helpful (and, of course, some rather unhelpful) comments, and the overall sense of the importance of process and enfranchisement into the many-layered development of writing is strengthened.

Wrap-Ups

If time allows, you can take advantage of two activities we've used successfully to bring student scoring to a close. One is to have students keep the last paper they've read and dramatically unveil the final score it received from adults. You can ask for a show of hands of scores that were the same or were within a half-point difference. (This is an instant indicator of how student scores corresponded—or didn't—to teacher scores.) It's fun for students to see how closely their scores matched.

Another closure activity is to have a few students read aloud the last paper they scored without announcing what score it's been given. You can lead a discussion of the salient characteristics of each paper, asking class members to assert (and justify by using language from the rubric) the score they'd have given it. Then ask the student reader to reveal the score it received. Again, this gives students immediate feedback on their interpretation of the rubric, and we find it is a strong motivator in getting students to improve their writing.

Having students score papers is an effective way of helping them internalize features of the rubric and exposing them to different writing approaches. There's a problem, of course, if the students are far off in their evaluation—even if the teacher's score is corrective—the student writer gets a false sense of just where a given paper lines up with the rubric score points. Giving students (as with adult scorers) multiple opportunities to score papers helps them achieve progressively closer alignment to the rubric.

THE POWER OF STUDENT EXAMPLES

Student examples—anchor papers or any other examples, whether from past years or from other classes this year—are powerful. A rubric, though important, can be too abstract for students. An essay that illustrates the rubric is exponentially more powerful than a list of characteristics of a good essay or a list of shoulds. The more high-quality student examples a student can be exposed to, the more quickly that student's writing will improve.

How to make this available? Certainly making copies of anchor packets and discussing each paper in great detail is powerful. So can a pass-around of essays—voluntary, of course, by students of the class. (Will reading high-quality papers by other students spur the reader to emulate the style of those high-scoring students? Probably. Nothing's wrong with that! They're trying their wings and doing only what all the other original writers in history have done at some point in their careers, and a few borrowed feathers will do them no harm.)

LOOK FOR PATTERNS

Look for patterns—you'll see them, and you'll build lessons around them. We list a variety of useful mini-lesson topics here to get you thinking about follow-up instruction and alert you to the wide range of departure points that offer students focused practice at writing improvement. In a class of English-language learners, for example, students might be strong on energy and enthusiasm, but have real problems with subject-verb agreement and plurals. Structure future lessons on those issues. Basic classes will also have work to do on paragraphing, for many students either forget or do not know how or when to break paragraphs. The same is true of giving titles: some students forget titles entirely, and titles can be powerful.

Many classes will have work to do on the difference between an essay and a journal entry; on magnetic openings; strong introductory paragraphs; careful development; fitting conclusions; voice; logical sequence; issues of relevance versus irrelevance; and strategies such as the use of dialogue, the felicitous citation of examples, and inclusion of counter-arguments. Most classes will also have work to do on description. You'll build lessons around those issues, too, reminding students that most unskilled writers stick to visual description, and that one mark of a good writer is exploitation of more of the five senses. We have included two worksheets to guide revision (and subsequent composing) in Appendix B: "Narrative Writing Strategies" and Appendix C: "Persuasive Writing Pitfalls." Distribute these to students as their genre repertoire expands and as their writing becomes more sophisticated.

Students will benefit from work on avoiding sentence-type repetition. A mini-lesson on sentence combining can show students the myriad possibilities of building elegant structure. Teachers may also want to work on issues such as overuse of passive voice, consistency of logic, effective or gratuitous use of quotations, or effective or ineffective service of metaphor (clichés, mixed metaphors, single powerful metaphors woven throughout essays). *You will want to design mini-lessons based on the writing strategy that gives your students the most bang for their buck.* Which two or three focus areas would help most students significantly improve their essays? Choose those to teach.

Scoring Guide for Revising Your Writing About a Place

Five Features of Descriptive Writing
• Description • Organization of Ideas • Writer's Voice
• Language: Sentences and Vocabulary • Mechanics: Spelling and Grammar

If your score was...	*Choose three features to revise...*
1 • DEVELOPING • Description is vague or incomplete; writing may be only a list without elaboration. • Introduction, middle, or conclusion may be unclear or missing; extremely brief. • Writing does not show writer's personality or tell why place is meaningful. • Language may be general and vague, or there may be incomplete or run-on sentences. • Errors may make it difficult for reader to understand ideas.	
2 • NEARLY PROFICIENT • Description is underdeveloped and may not be clear; reader has questions. • Place is introduced, but writing moves too fast; conclusion may be abrupt or missing. • Writing may not seem connected to writer through any sense of voice. • Language is simple; sentence types are mostly the same or simple; vocabulary is limited. • Writing shows limited control of conventions; errors are distracting.	
3 • PROFICIENT • Description is clear and elaborated; the reader has a complete picture of the place though there may be more "telling" than "showing." • There is a clear beginning, middle, and conclusion, and writing includes transitions from one part to another. • Writing reflects author's thoughts and feelings directly or indirectly. • Language is clear; some sentence variety; vocabulary is general rather than specific. • Writing shows control of writing conventions; errors do not interfere with meaning.	
4 • COMMENDABLE • Description is vivid and well elaborated through a variety of descriptive strategies such as images, anecdotes, and illustrative details that enable the reader to clearly imagine the place. • Beginning is engaging and description is presented in a clever or unusual way; conclusion ties elements of description together. • Writing reflects author's thoughts and feelings through commentary, interior monologue, dialogue, description of thoughts or feelings, or by directly addressing the reader. • Language is lively and expressive; sentences are varied; vocabulary is rich and precise. • Writing shows mastery of mechanics, though there may be a few errors.	

REWRITES!

Many possibilities exist. Aside from (and perhaps after) the kind of ad hoc prescriptive lessons just described, why not structure your plans so that students can write their essays over? One approach to having students rewrite is to present them with a "Reverse Rubric" (shown on p. 55) in which they use the descriptors from the next higher level to guide the revisions they make. Joe, for example, who got a 2 on his essay about his personal oasis (Lesson 1) will use the descriptors of a 3 paper to make changes as he rewrites, using the reformatted rubric. Use the "Reverse Rubric" model to guide revision for other genres and different topics.

Peer review can be integrated into the process of revision, and lots of class discussion and Writer's Workshop–style collaboration can ensue. (Not realistic given the time pressures your district exerts on you? Do a few follow-up mini-lessons, schedule some practice for homework, and have students rewrite their essays as a homework assignment as well.)

You can see that students' completed essays, then, can be used as precious mines whose ore can be processed into effective lessons—lessons applicable to your class.

Finally, just a reiteration that follow-up writing assessments are the only way to chart real progress during the year and over the years. One hopes, of course, that a student's holistic score will inch its way up—sometimes, of course, dropping back temporarily, and students should be apprised of that possibility. Your careful charting of those scores will also give you an idea of whether your teaching is showing results.

 **PART TWO** The Lessons

Note to Teachers: Feel free to photocopy and distribute pages from the lessons as well as the Rubric Tip Sheet (pages 27 and 28) and the Scoring Guides. You will want to enlarge pages slightly to give students more space for jotting notes, writing, and drawing.

A Personal Oasis

Most of us are very busy. With school and work, we have a lot to do, but we all need places to go in our worlds and in our minds where we can feel calm and comfortable. These places help us with the stress of a busy life.

An oasis is a place in a desert with water and trees. In other words, it's a pleasant place. Some of us have literal oases, places where we go to relax. Some of us have figurative oases, activities we do or thoughts we have to relax. We all need to escape sometimes.

Sometimes we escape by playing a game or watching a TV show. Other times we escape by thinking of imaginary people, places, or events. Sometimes we have special places where we go to have time to ourselves. This lesson gives you an opportunity to imagine a special place, and then practice your writing skills by describing it.

GETTING STARTED

To begin, visualize a real or imaginary place that could be your own personal oasis. What does it look like? Where is it located? What do you hear and see there? How does this place make you feel? Draw a picture of this place in the space below.

A Sketch of My Personal Oasis

READING

Now read the poem "I Have an Oasis" by Colin McNaughton. As you read, look for details, and think about how the oasis in the poem is similar to or different from the one you drew.

I Have an Oasis
By Colin McNaughton

I have an oasis,
It's up in the clouds,
Away from the rush
And the roar of the crowds,
Away from the pushing
And pulling and pain,
Away from the sadness
And anger and strain,
Away from the envy
And cheating and greed,
Away from the pressure—
What more could I need?
I grow my geraniums
And lettuce that's curled,
In my little garden
On top of the world.

THINKING AND TALKING

After reading, complete the following exercises with a classmate.

1. Where is Colin's oasis?

_____

_____

_____

2. What is something you will find in Colin's oasis?

_____

_____

_____

3. What are three things you *won't* find in Colin's oasis?

_____

_____

_____

4. Why do you think Colin has an oasis?

_____

_____

_____

5. Put a check next to the questions below that Colin answers:

☐ a. Where is this special place? ☐ b. When or why does the writer go to this place? ☐ c. What or who is in this place? ☐ d. What or who is not in this place?

☐ e. What does the writer do here? ☐ f. How is the writer comforted in this place? ☐ g. What sounds, sights, or sensations does the writer find here? ☐ h. What does the writer think about here?

6. Finally, draw a picture of Colin's oasis as you see it in your mind:

Colin's Oasis

PLANNING

Now develop your ideas for writing about your personal oasis. Go back to the drawing you created in the "Getting Started" section. Add more details to your drawing and write word labels on what you drew. This will help you generate vocabulary for the writing you'll do later. When you have done that, answer the following questions (you will recognize them from the "Thinking and Talking" section), and extend and develop your ideas by adding examples, comparisons, and vivid descriptions of what you see, hear, and feel. When you write, put them in the order you see here, or, if you like, change the order of ideas. Remember to include "showing" language.

Your Personal Oasis Planning Guide

Where is this special place? How did you create or discover this place?	When or why do you go to this place?	What or who is in this place?	What or who is not in this place?
What do you do here?	How are you comforted in this place?	What sounds, sights, or sensations do you find here?	What do you think about here?

> ### *Writing Prompt: A Personal Oasis*
>
> Write about a personal oasis—a place that helps you relax and that you know well. It can be real or it can be a place in your mind. Write about what you see and hear and feel in this place. Describe this place so that the reader can easily imagine being there and give the reader a sense of when you like to go there.

REVISING AND EDITING

After writing, review this checklist and make necessary changes.

- ☐ Did you present a place by using some of these descriptive strategies: specific details about what you see, hear, or feel; images; anecdotes?
- ☐ Did you include specific description (facts, images, dialogue, actions, behavior, comparison)?
- ☐ Did you include what you think about and how you feel in your oasis?
- ☐ Did you include why this is a personal oasis?
- ☐ How about the ending? Did you close your piece?
- ☐ Did you vary your sentence types and use vivid and precise vocabulary?
- ☐ Check your punctuation. Did you use capital letters, commas, periods, and quotation marks where they belong?
- ☐ Review your grammar: Do subjects and verbs agree? Check for other grammar trouble-spots you want to correct.
- ☐ Did you title your essay to give the reader an idea of what to expect?

SELF-ASSESSMENT

Congratulations on completing this process. How would you score this piece of writing?

☐ (4) Commendable   ☐ (3) Proficient   ☐ (2) Nearly Proficient   ☐ (1) Developing

Scoring Guide for Lesson 1: A Personal Oasis

GENRE: WRITING ABOUT A PLACE

> ### *Five Features of Descriptive Writing*
> - Description
> - Organization of Ideas
> - Writer's Voice
> - Language: Sentences and Vocabulary
> - Mechanics: Spelling and Grammar

4 • COMMENDABLE

- Description is vivid and well elaborated through a variety of descriptive strategies such as images, anecdotes, and illustrative details that enable the reader to clearly imagine the place.
- Beginning is engaging and description is presented in a clever or unusual way; conclusion ties elements of description together.
- Writing reflects author's thoughts and feelings through commentary, interior monologue, dialogue, description of thoughts or feelings, or by directly addressing the reader.
- Language is lively and expressive; sentences are varied; vocabulary is rich and precise.
- Writing shows mastery of mechanics, though there may be a few errors.

3 • PROFICIENT

- Description is clear and elaborated; the reader has a complete picture of the place, though there may be more "telling" than "showing."
- There is a clear beginning, middle, and conclusion, and writing includes transitions from one part to another.
- Writing reflects author's thoughts and feelings directly or indirectly.
- Language is clear; some sentence variety; vocabulary is general rather than specific.
- Writing shows control of writing conventions; errors do not interfere with meaning.

2 • NEARLY PROFICIENT

- Description is underdeveloped and may not be clear; reader has questions.
- Place is introduced, but writing moves too fast; conclusion may be abrupt or missing.
- Writing may not seem connected to writer through any sense of voice.
- Language is simple; sentence types are mostly the same or simple; vocabulary is limited.
- Writing shows limited control of conventions; errors are distracting.

1 • DEVELOPING

- Description is vague or incomplete; writing may be only a list without elaboration.
- Introduction, middle, or conclusion may be unclear or missing; extremely brief.
- Writing does not show writer's personality or tell why place is meaningful.
- Language may be general and vague, or there may be incomplete or run-on sentences.
- Errors may make it difficult for reader to understand ideas.

A Childhood Passion

When you were younger, did you have ideas about what you wanted to be when you grew up? Did you want to be a sports hero? A movie star? A video game designer? Many of us have aspirations when we're young—and for some of us, they come true.

In this lesson you'll have a chance to remember and write about what you wanted to do or be when you were younger. You'll include characters and action and details that show what you saw or heard or felt. Try to write about this time in your life so that the reader can easily imagine what you did and how you felt.

GETTING STARTED

To begin, think of what you most wanted to do or be when you were younger. Begin to elaborate on this time in your life by taking notes below.

When you were younger, what did you want to BE? Why?

When you were younger, what did you want to DO? Why?

What kinds of things did you do or imagine you could do to make this come true?

READING

Read "Lash La Rue," by Jerry Spinelli, a popular children's book author. In this selection, Spinelli describes the characters he admired when he was really young.

Lash La Rue

By Jerry Spinelli

Early on I learned, without anyone actually telling me, that in this world it is not enough just to be. You have to be something.

So around the age of five I decided to be a cowboy. Cowboys rode three trails into my life: (1) The Garrick Movie Theater downtown, which showed Western double features on Saturday afternoon, (2) comic books, and (3) "Frontier Playhouse."

"Frontier Playhouse" came on TV every weeknight at six, right after "Howdy Doody" and right in the middle of dinnertime. I was not allowed to eat in the living room, where the TV was, but I was allowed to move my chair to the doorway between the kitchen and dining room. I placed my dinner on the seat, knelt down, and watched the nightly cowboy movie while eating on my knees. It's a wonder I could see the platter-size screen at the far end of the house.

From TV and movies and comics I knew lots of cowboys: Roy Rogers, Gene Autry, Hopalong Cassidy, Lash La Rue, Red Ryder, Tom Mix, the Lone Ranger, Tex Ritter, Ranger Joe, Tim McCoy, Hoot Gibson. And horses: Trigger, Topper, Silver, Champion, Tony, Buttermilk.

When my friends and I played cowboys, almost everyone wanted to be Roy Rogers. With his fringed shirts and silky neckerchief and white hat and golden horse, how could you not want to be Roy? I was usually the first to call out, "I'll be Roy Rogers!"

But when I was alone and my secrets came peeping out from their hiding places, I knew there was a cowboy I wanted to be even more than Roy Rogers. I wanted to be Lash La Rue. From hat to boots, Lash La Rue dressed all in black. But that wasn't what made Lash La Rue special—it was the whip. He carried it coiled at his belt, and with it he did most everything the others did with their six-shooters. Was a bad guy reaching for his gun? Lash was quicker with his whip. A flick of the wrist, the whip uncoils— leather lightning!—darts ten, twenty, thirty feet across the dust to snatch the gun, barely clear of its holster, from the bad guy's hand. Is the bad guy running away? The whip catches him at the ankles, trips and hogties him, ready for the sheriff. The rawhide tongue could lick the spit from a horse's lips or kiss it on the ear.

Lash La Rue. I recognized him as "cool" before I ever knew the word.

THINKING AND TALKING

Work with a partner to answer these questions.

1. Do you know about any famous cowboys? Share what you know about them.

_____

_____

_____

2. What did the writer decide to be and when? Why?

_____

_____

_____

_____

3. How did the writer learn about cowboys?

_____

_____

_____

_____

4. Why did the writer especially admire Lash La Rue?

_____

_____

_____

_____

5. Fill in the details about Lash here:

What did he wear?

What could he do?

_____

_____

_____

_____

6. What did Lash represent to the writer?

_____

_____

_____

_____

7. Compare your childhood passion to Spinelli's. How are they similar? How are they different?

_____

_____

_____

_____

PLANNING

Now develop details about the childhood passion you have thought about and chosen to write about. Use questions from the reading to help you.

A Childhood Passion Planning Guide

1. What did you want to do or be when you were younger?

2. When did you decide this? Why?

3. How did you learn about your childhood passion?

4. What did others say to you at this time?

5. Give some details about your childhood passion. If you chose to resemble a person, describe the person. If you chose a game or activity, describe the activity.

6. What did this childhood passion represent to you?

> ### *Writing Prompt: A Childhood Passion*
>
> Write about a hero or a job or a game or an activity you were passionate about when you were younger. Describe why you developed the passion and what you imagined or did or believed. Did other friends or family members know about it? If so, what did they say to you, or how did they react? What did the childhood passion represent for you? Use descriptive details, dialogue, vivid vocabulary, and interior monologue to help the reader imagine this time in your life.

REVISING AND EDITING

After writing, review this checklist and make necessary changes.

- ☐ Did you begin with a "magnetic" introduction that gives some background about you when you were young?

- ☐ Did you include specific details about when and where this interest began?

- ☐ Did you explain how you learned about your passion and how it developed?

- ☐ Did you describe who was there and what they said or thought?

- ☐ Did you include interior monologue (what you were thinking)?

- ☐ Did you write about what this childhood passion represented for you?

- ☐ Did you organize the descriptions and events of your story into paragraphs?

- ☐ Check your punctuation. Did you use capital letters, commas, periods, and quotation marks where they belong?

- ☐ Did you add an enticing title to make the reader want to learn more?

SELF-ASSESSMENT

Congratulations on completing this process. How would you score this piece of writing?

☐ (4) Commendable   ☐ (3) Proficient   ☐ (2) Nearly Proficient   ☐ (1) Developing

Scoring Guide for Lesson 2:
A Childhood Passion

GENRE: PERSONAL NARRATION

Five Features in Personal Narrative Writing
- Presentation and Development of the Experience
- Organization of Ideas
- Writer's Voice
- Language: Sentences and Vocabulary
- Mechanics: Spelling and Grammar

---

4 • COMMENDABLE
- Writing presents a past interest, person, or activity in an original or clever way and uses descriptive strategies such as images, anecdotes, and illustrative details that enable the reader to learn about the writer's experiences.
- Beginning engages reader, middle develops ideas, and conclusion fits.
- The writer's personality emerges from the writing through interior monologue, dialogue, description of thoughts or feelings, or by directly addressing the reader.
- Language is generally precise and lively. Sentences are varied and vocabulary is specific.
- Writing shows clear control of writing conventions; errors do not cause confusion.

3 • PROFICIENT
- Presents a past experience and includes elaboration, though the reader may have questions; writing has some "showing," though there may be more "telling."
- Has a clear beginning, middle, and conclusion.
- Writing helps reader get to know the writer.
- Language is clear, but sentence types may not be varied; vocabulary is general.
- Writing shows control of writing conventions; errors do not interfere with meaning.

2 • NEARLY PROFICIENT
- Describes a past experience incompletely; examples may seem not directly related or unbelievable, or they may be missing.
- Experience is introduced, but piece moves too fast; conclusion may be abrupt or missing.
- Writing does not capture the personality of the writer.
- Language is simple; sentence types are mostly the same; vocabulary is limited.
- Errors may be distracting.

1 • DEVELOPING
- Past experience is vague or incomplete; may be a list without examples.
- Brief introduction, limited elaboration, and conclusion may be missing.
- Writing does not show writer's personality.
- Language is general and vague, or there may be incomplete or run-on sentences.
- Errors may make it difficult for reader to understand ideas.

Something About Me You May Not Know

Here's a chance to practice your writing skills and tell the reader something about yourself. Your writing will be scored, and you'll learn what some of your strengths are and what you can improve.

Most people find it easy to write about themselves. This prompt invites you to present yourself in a new and different way. The reader will learn something new about you—and you just may learn something new about yourself too!

GETTING STARTED

To begin, think about a few things your friends may not know about you. These may be a funny habit, a secret wish, or a special skill. In the space below, jot down a few things about yourself that your friends don't know. You can make a list, write sentences, or draw.

Some Things My Friends Don't Know About Me

You're going to read "Star Boy," a story about a Native American boy who lives with his family on an island. You'll notice that through his writing, he talks directly to the reader. We learn that he thinks his sister is bossy and that he has lots of questions about who he is, where he lives, and what things mean. As you read "Star Boy," look for what he tells us about himself directly and indirectly through his story.

READING

Read "Star Boy." If possible, ask your teacher or a classmate to read this aloud, since it is a particularly nice selection to listen to.

Star Boy
By Michael Dorris

You know how it is when you're on the beach on a white sunny morning and you shut your eyes tight? What you see isn't exactly dark, at least not dark the way it's dark when you're inside your house at night and you can't make anything out, when every noise is a question you can't answer. What you see with your eyes closed during the day is something different. It's like deep water, a pond that's draped with shade. I don't know what makes it happen—the fins of tiny fish, or their eyes, the sparkle of agates—but there are lights moving down there, something to watch. It's the same on a night when there's no moon and you look straight into the sky: the more you watch, the more you see. Grains of white sand, it looks like, and sometimes one drops so fast you can hardly follow it before it's lost.

What I don't like is nothing. I don't mean I like everything, because I don't. I don't like it when my sister wakes me up. I don't like to eat fish with too many bones. I don't like those hungry bugs so small you don't know they're there until they bite you. But mostly I don't like . . . nothing. You know: *nothing*. I don't like it when there's nothing to hear, nothing to taste, nothing to touch, especially when there's nothing to see. Those times, I don't know where I am. The first night I woke up and noticed that everyone was invisible, I held perfectly still and disappeared. I became nothing, too, and I didn't know how to get back. Finally I talked to myself, whispered a little song my father sings when he speaks to the birds, excusing himself for bothering them. I rubbed the tip of my thumb against the tip of my fingers. I touched my tongue to my lips and tasted salt from the ocean, and I waited that way until the day remembered us, and returned.

"Why are you awake so early?" my mother asked me that morning. "Are you becoming the same kind of flower as your sister, the kind that bends to the east and calls the sun?"

I didn't like being anything like my sister, who in fact is called Morning Girl because she gets up before everyone else, so I told a different story.

"I don't need sleep anymore," I said.

"That's too bad." My mother shook her head and smoothed my hair flat. "How will you dream if you don't sleep? How will you hear yourself?"

I thought about this problem.

"Maybe you're a bat," my mother suggested, smiling at me, "and will dream all day while the rest of us work. How lucky for you."

I thought of bats and how they race through the dark sky fast as late summer rain. I thought of how the wind would feel against my skin if I could fly.

"It's true," I said. "I *will* sleep today."

"And hang upside down from the limb of a tree?" asked Morning Girl, who always listened to what anyone said even though it had nothing to do with her. "I want to see that. Maybe I'll poke you with a stick."

"And maybe during the night I'll land in your hair," I told her. "Maybe I'll build a nest."

"Bats don't make nests," she pointed out, but still she raised her hand to her head at the idea.

"Maybe I'm a new kind of bat."

"What is it about the night that you like?" my mother asked, to stop the argument—but not just for that reason. She was truly interested and always listened closely to what I said. Now she stopped cleaning a manioc root and looked at me.

"I like . . .," I began, and thought back to the white sand scattered on the sky's black beach. "I like the stars. I like to look down at them."

"You don't look *down* at the sky," Morning Girl contradicted. "You look up."

"Maybe not if you're a bat," my father said, his voice very serious. His eyes were still closed, and so it seemed as though his words came from nowhere. We couldn't tell if he was joking or not. "But no one is asking the right question," he continued. "Why *don't* bats sleep at night? Perhaps they like the same things as this Star Boy does."

Star Boy.

That was the first time I heard my new name. Star Boy. Before that I was called "Hungry" because that's what I was most of the time. I like "Star Boy" much better. No one spoke as we all listened, test the weight of the words.

Star Boy.

My mother smiled. "Who is talking?" she asked at last. "Who has found such a good question? Who has thought of such a fine name for my son?"

"It is the father of a bat," said my father. "The father of a morning flower. It is the husband of the mother of a bat and a flower. It is a man who is surrounded by people who talk when others are trying the sleep. I think I must be in the wrong family, since I am the only one who knows the value of rest. I think—"

My mother looked at Morning Girl and me with her eyebrows raised, then slipped a piece of clean fruit between my father's lips to stop his words. We all watched while he chewed. He still did not open his eyes.

"No," he said after he swallowed. "This is not the wrong family. There is only one person who knows where to find fruit so sweet, only one person with fingers so gentle."

My mother lowered her eyes, but she was pleased. "Why do bats like the dark?" she asked me, returning to our conversation. "Tell us, Star Boy."

When she used my new name I knew it was now mine for good, and at that moment I decided that I would become an expert, a person who would be asked questions about the night and who would know the answers.

"Because it's big," I said. "Because there are special things to see if you watch closely. Because in it you can be dreaming even if you're awake. Because someone must remember the day while others sleep and call it when it's time for the sun to come home."

My father opened his eyes at last, propped himself on his elbows, and nodded.

"Star Boy," he said.

THINKING AND TALKING

After reading, work with a partner to answer these questions.

1. Star Boy uses lots of *images* (pictures) to describe what he thinks about. What are some of the images you remember from the story?

_____

_____

_____

_____

2. What are five things you learned about Star Boy?

_____

_____

_____

_____

3. Which words would you choose to describe Star Boy's sister? What about his mother? His father?

_____

_____

_____

_____

4. What was Star Boy's previous name? Why did he have that name?

_____

_____

_____

_____

5. Do you think Star Boy is a good name for the character you met in the story? Why?

_____

_____

_____

_____

6. Why does Star Boy compare himself to a bat?

_____

_____

_____

_____

7. Based on who you are and what you're interested in, what new name would you choose for yourself? Why?

_____

_____

_____

_____

8. Based on who you are and what you're interested in, what animal would you compare yourself to?

_____

_____

_____

_____

PLANNING

Just as Star Boy revealed some information about himself in the reading, you're going to tell the reader something about yourself. Choose one of the topics in the center box in the Planning Chart:

- a new name for yourself or an animal you are like, or

- something about you that others do not know

Circle your topic. Answer questions in each box to develop details for your writing, jotting additional notes at the bottom of the page.

Planning Chart for Writing About Yourself

What do you love to do? What do your interests or hobbies reveal about you?	What time of day do you prefer? When are you most relaxed? Productive? Energetic?		What are your goals? What do you want to do in life?
Who are your closest friends? Why? What does your choice of friends reveal about you?	**Your New Name or an Animal You're Like**	**Something About You Others Don't Know**	How do you get along with members of your family?
What do you think about? What do you dream about? What do your thoughts and dreams reveal about you?	Something else?		What is really, really important to you? What could you not live without?

> ### *Writing Prompt: Something About Me You May Not Know*
>
> Select one of these topics.
> - Topic 1: Choose a new name for yourself. Perhaps that name includes an animal or animal attributes. Explain what events or flashes of recognition brought you to this new name, and how this new name describes something important about who you are. Let the reader get to know this new you.
> - Topic 2: Many people know many things about you, but there are lots of things that even people close to you don't know. Choose something that others may not know about you, and write about it showing the reader how this interest or aspect of your personality developed, and what it says about who you are and will be in the future.

REVISING AND EDITING

After writing, review this checklist and make necessary changes.

- ☐ Did you begin your personal description in an interesting or unusual way?
- ☐ Did you include enough information? Does the reader learn something new about you? Did you include some of these:
  - ☐ Something you love to do
  - ☐ Your favorite time of day
  - ☐ Your goals
  - ☐ Your best friends
  - ☐ How you and your family members get along
  - ☐ What you think or dream about
  - ☐ What is important to you
  - ☐ What some or all of these things reveal about you
- ☐ Did you include images to help the reader imagine scenes, people, or animals?
- ☐ Did you organize your main ideas into paragraphs? (You remembered to indent the first line of each paragraph, right?)
- ☐ Check your punctuation. Did you use capital letters, commas, periods, and quotation marks where they belong?
- ☐ How about the ending? Do you bring everything together at the end?
- ☐ Did you title your essay?

SELF-ASSESSMENT

Congratulations on completing this process. How would you score this piece of writing?

☐ (4) Commendable   ☐ (3) Proficient   ☐ (2) Nearly Proficient   ☐ (1) Developing

Scoring Guide for Lesson 3: Something About Me You May Not Know

GENRE: PERSONAL DESCRIPTION

Five Features of Personal Description Writing
- The Personal Description: Development and Clarity
- Organization of Ideas
- Writer's Voice
- Language: Sentences and Vocabulary
- Mechanics: Spelling and Grammar

---

4 • COMMENDABLE
- Presents a personal description in a clever and elaborated way; uses a variety of strategies such as use of images, anecdotes, or specific details that enable the reader to get to know the writer.
- Beginning engages reader, middle develops ideas, and conclusion fits.
- The writer's personality emerges from the writing through interior monologue, dialogue, description of thoughts or feelings, or directly addressing the reader.
- Language is generally lively; sentences are varied, and vocabulary is precise.
- Writing shows clear control of writing conventions; errors do not cause confusion.

3 • PROFICIENT
- Presents a personal description and includes elaboration, though the reader may have questions; writing has some "showing," though there may be more "telling."
- Has a clear beginning, middle, and conclusion.
- Writing helps reader get to know the writer.
- Language is clear. Sentence types may not be varied; vocabulary is generally descriptive.
- Writing shows control of writing conventions; errors do not interfere with meaning.

2 • NEARLY PROFICIENT
- Description is incomplete; examples may seem artificial or unbelievable.
- Person is introduced, but piece moves too fast; conclusion may be abrupt or missing.
- Writing does not reflect the personality of the writer.
- Language is basic; sentence types are mostly simple or the same; vocabulary is limited.
- Errors may be distracting.

1 • DEVELOPING
- Personal description is vague or incomplete; few details are provided.
- Brief introduction, limited elaboration, and conclusion may be missing.
- Writing does not show writer's personality.
- Language is unclear or vague, or there may be incomplete or run-on sentences.
- Errors may make it difficult for reader to understand ideas.

Something I'll Never Forget

For each of us, there are some events that we will never forget. Sometimes these are happy memories, sometimes they're funny, or sometimes even frightening or sad.

In this lesson, you'll practice your skills at describing a specific event from your past. You'll want to include characters and action and details that show what you experienced—saw or heard or felt. Try to write about the event so that the reader can easily imagine what happened and why you remember it.

GETTING STARTED

To begin, think of several events you will never forget. Take a few minutes to draw or write about them in the space below.

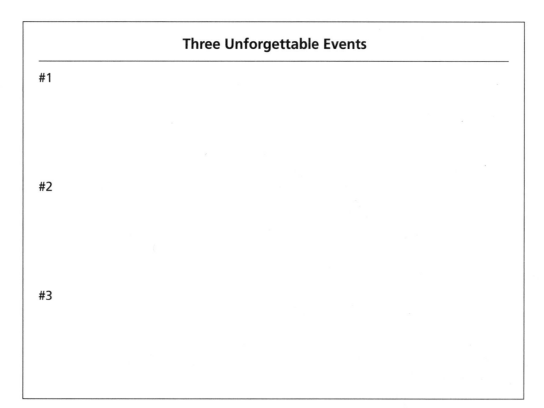

Three Unforgettable Events

#1

#2

#3

Now talk with a partner about your memorable events. Ask and answer some of these questions:

Where were you?

How old were you?

What happened?

How did you feel?

If you were trying to learn something, what was it?

READING

In this excerpt, the writer describes an annual ritual that still haunts him. As you read, look for where the writer (1) compares one thing to another, (2) tells you what he's thinking, and (3) describes his feelings. In case you wonder about it, the "Hanon" that the writer mentions partway through was someone who composed difficult practice drills for music students.

Musical Ordeal

By Thad Carhart

The first year that I went through this ordeal—I was nine years old—I didn't suspect what was in store until I actually entered the big room that was the parlor, dressed in a blazer, with my hair slicked down. Then and only then did I experience firsthand the controlled terror of my peers: the stiff-legged walk to the front of the room, the explosion of sound from the big piano against a soundless gathering, the smattering of applause, and the rapid repetition of the sequence with the next student. To say that I panicked is too simple to describe what happened.

"Now we'll have an early Beethoven piece from Thad Carhart," I heard Miss Pemberton say, and only dimly did I connect that name with my own. My legs carried me uncertainly up the narrow aisle that threaded through the parents and siblings of my fellow students, and I sat down on the piano bench. A strange giddiness possessed me, as if I might start pounding the keyboard at random and expect it to pass for a difficult piece, and my own piece, the real one, was as alien to me as the dark side of the moon. *How does it go?* I asked myself. *How, at least, does it begin?* My features were frozen in a rictus of false enthusiasm and my fingers rolled into fists as if they were retractable. After many motionless seconds, Miss Pemberton came over from her place at the side and, with the pretext that the height of the bench needed to be adjusted, she screened me from the audience and hissed in my ear as she leaned over, "It starts with a C-minor chord." I looked at her with no hint of comprehension in my eyes, and she placed her right hand on the keyboard and played the chord softly, as if she were checking that the piano was in tune. The instant I heard those notes the spell was broken. *I know that piece!* I thought to myself, and as my eyes brightened her hand patted me firmly on the back. She moved away and I attacked the keys as if they were the enemy, playing the piece straight through without a mistake. That is, I played all of the notes, but I must have taken it at double the usual tempo with no regard whatsoever for phrasing, much less interpretation, When I finished I felt the way a circus animal must feel that has just successfully performed a particularly difficult and silly trick, and my sense of disappointment matched my surprise that such a big deal was made of this strange ceremony.

I played in two more of Miss Pemberton's recitals, but each time it was like holding my breath and swimming underwater until I reached the other side, the end of the piece. Hanon, I suppose it should be said, never did let me down: my fingers were nimble, my retention was good, but there was never for me a feeling of the music coming back to me. It was an ordeal that had to be tolerated so that I could continue to learn to play music for myself.

These kinds of recitals seem to me to be based on an enormous confidence game that sets up every prospective pianist to be the next Horowitz. Only a handful of soloists will, of course, rise to the top and make careers out of their music, but the conceit is that any talented youngster might have this capacity, this dubious and rare gift. And so there has developed over many years a system for subjecting thousands upon thousands of young musicians to the ordeal of playing repeatedly in public to see if they have the peculiar sort of talent that flourishes in front of others.

I didn't have that talent, that much was clear, but that awareness didn't diminish my eagerness to keep learning: I always enjoyed playing on my own. For as long as I took lessons as a child, I gently but persistently resisted the notion that I should play in front of others and, while this attitude was tolerated, I was made to understand that I wasn't really playing the game. My parents never pushed me; five children in a household have a way of defusing the pressure to perform that might otherwise come their way. Mostly I think this was just understood to be part of the system of taking lessons and no one thought to approach music otherwise. Only one or two of Miss Pemberton's students seemed drawn to performing for others, and they were the ones who were most advanced and who were likely to center their lives around music. To the rest of us the recitals were a strange amalgam: half exam, half carnival, with a dreadful thrill of anticipation until the awful night slowly arrived and quickly passed. I sometimes dream about those strange evening encounters; I always forget how my piece begins and Miss Pemberton is nowhere to be found.

THINKING AND TALKING

Work with a partner to answer these questions about "Musical Ordeal."

1. What was most memorable to you about the story?

_____

_____

_____

2. Where and when did the event happen?

_____

_____

_____

3. Who are the two main characters? Give two details about each of them.

Character #1: _____

Details: _____

_____

_____

_____

Character #2: _____

Details: _____

_____

_____

_____

4. Choose a sentence about each of the main characters and note what it reveals about the character.

Sentence	What this reveals about the character
Character #1	
Character #2	

5. Look for two places where the writer compares one thing to another. Record them here.

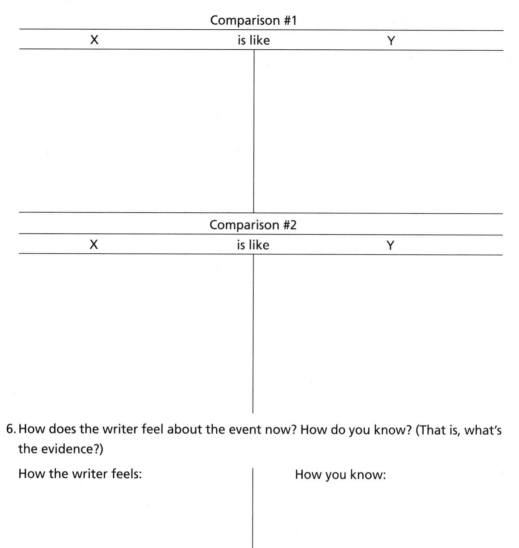

Comparison #1

X	is like	Y

Comparison #2

X	is like	Y

6. How does the writer feel about the event now? How do you know? (That is, what's the evidence?)

How the writer feels:

How you know:

7. How do the author's descriptive details "show" or connect his experiences with his thoughts and feelings?

Descriptive details   →   Thoughts and feelings

PLANNING

Now choose an unforgettable event of your own to write about. Develop details about the memory by answering questions in the planning guide.

Unforgettable Event Planning Guide

1. Where and when did the event happen?
   _____

2. Who was present? Give some details about each character.
   Character #1:
   _____
   _____
   _____

   Character #2:
   _____
   _____
   _____

   Character #3:
   _____
   _____
   _____

3. What did the characters say or do? Use quotes or sentences to reveal something important about the characters.

Character	Quotation/Sentence	What this reveals about the character
•		
•		
•		

4. Use comparisons to help the reader imagine your experience.

Comparison		
X	is like	Y
•		
•		

5. How do you feel about the event now? What is something that shows how you feel?

How you feel:	Something that *shows* how you feel:

> ### *Writing Prompt: Something I'll Never Forget*
>
> Write about an event you will never forget, whether that event occurred recently or a long time ago. Use a few narrative strategies (descriptive details, dialogue, interior monologue, comparisons, and specific vocabulary, for example) to help the reader imagine the incident.

REVISING AND EDITING

After writing, review this checklist and make necessary changes.

- ☐ Did you let the reader know where and when the event occurred?
- ☐ Did you include specific details about why the event happened?
- ☐ Did you describe who was there?
- ☐ Did you include dialogue?
- ☐ Did you include interior monologue (what you were thinking)?
- ☐ Did you use comparisons to help the reader visualize details?
- ☐ Did you describe your feelings at the time of the event?
- ☐ Did you show what happened at the end?
- ☐ Did you organize your narrative into paragraphs?
- ☐ Did you describe how and why you remember this event now?
- ☐ Check your punctuation. Did you use capital letters, commas, periods, and quotation marks where they belong?
- ☐ Did you add an interesting title to make the reader want to read about your memory?

SELF-ASSESSMENT

Congratulations on completing this process. How would you score this piece of writing?

☐ (4) Commendable   ☐ (3) Proficient   ☐ (2) Nearly Proficient   ☐ (1) Developing

Scoring Guide for Lesson 4:
Something I'll Never Forget

GENRE: PERSONAL NARRATION

Five Features in Personal Narrative Writing

- Event: Narrative Description and Elaboration
- Organization of Ideas
- Writer's Voice
- Language: Sentences and Vocabulary
- Mechanics: Spelling and Grammar

---

4 • COMMENDABLE

- Event is presented in a clever and vivid way; includes elaboration through description, use of images, anecdotes, and specific details that enable the reader to experience the event; details are convincing.
- Beginning is engaging, middle and ending are complete, and parts of the event may be presented in an unusual way.
- Writer is engaged in telling the story for the reader; writer's personality emerges from the writing through interior monologue, dialogue, description of thoughts or feelings, or directly addressing the reader.
- Language is precise and lively; sentences are varied, and vocabulary is specific.
- Writing shows clear control of writing conventions; errors do not cause confusion.

3 • PROFICIENT

- Describes past experience and includes some elaboration though the reader may have questions; writing has some "showing," though there may be more "telling."
- Has a clear beginning, middle, and conclusion.
- Writer's engagement is clear; significance of event comes through in writing.
- Language is clear; sentence types are varied; vocabulary is general.
- Writing shows control of writing conventions; errors do not interfere with meaning.

2 • NEARLY PROFICIENT

- Describes a past event incompletely or presents more than one event.
- Description of event may move too fast; parts (middle, end) may be abrupt or missing.
- Connection between event and writer may not be clear.
- Language is simple; sentence types are mostly the same; vocabulary is limited.
- Writing does not always show control of conventions; errors may interfere with meaning.

1 • DEVELOPING

- Past experience may be vague, incomplete, or a list without examples.
- Organization is not clear; parts of beginning, middle, and end may be missing.
- Writing does not communicate meaning or significance of event for writer.
- Language is general and vague; sentences may be incomplete or run-on.
- Errors may interfere with meaning.

House on Fire

We all have difficult times at some point in our lives. Everyone struggles, even though sometimes in the middle of a problem it seems as if we are the only people alive to have such difficulties. This lesson gives you an opportunity to identify a difficult issue in your life and write about it. Writing about problems can help develop creative ways to solve them, or at least produce new ways to think about them.

GETTING STARTED

To begin, think of three times in your past when you had a problem and solved it. Jot these down in the space below.

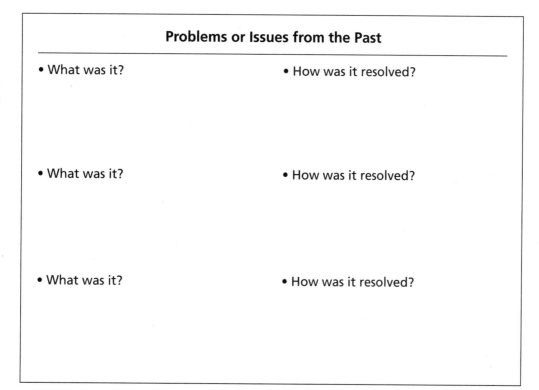

Problems or Issues from the Past	
• What was it?	• How was it resolved?
• What was it?	• How was it resolved?
• What was it?	• How was it resolved?

READING

Read "Forgiving Dad" by Erik Gundersen. In this story, the author describes a difficult issue in his life. As you read, look for answers to these questions:

- What is a "house on fire"?
- What is the writer's "house on fire"?
- Why does he want to write about his "house on fire" now?

Forgiving Dad

By Erik Gundersen

Sandra Cisneros, the writer, says that everyone has a house on fire. "Those things that are so taboo to you, so hidden from view, keep your house burning. Talk about them. Write about them," she told me and a group of colleagues at a teacher's conference last year. As I busily scribbled down these words of hers, these pearls of wisdom, I realized that my father was my house on fire. My troubled, angry, crazy, bitter relationship with him simmers, sparks, and sometimes even rages. And, for the most part, I just let it burn. But now, now that he's working so hard to gain my friendship, I have to decide if I want to forgive him.

When I was seven, my father told me that I was too big to hug him good-night. Ever since, I haven't really liked him that much. Throughout my early years, Dad was distant and sad, involved in a world of marriage and fatherhood that he wasn't ready to handle. His affection was so inconsistent and conditional that I knew not to trust him from an early age. I also knew that there were other differences between my dad and my friends' fathers. For one thing, theirs all seemed to have jobs, while mine didn't. In first grade, when Miss Cotter asked me what my father did, I sat speechless because I really didn't know. I felt my eyes fill with fear and shame.

Through my early adolescence, Dad drank a lot and spent money recklessly. And as Dad's behavior grew more and more unacceptable, my mother, brother, and I worked with increasing energy to shield him from outside scorn. Without ever discussing it, we began to tell carefully crafted stories designed to protect Dad from the questions and concerns of curious family members and friends.

My mother finally kicked Dad out of the house when I was seventeen, a senior in high school. Dad had done too many unspeakable things, worked too little, spent too much, and refused to acknowledge his drinking problem. Mom was tired of Dad's ways, sick of lying for him, ready for a new start. Or at least she thought she was. During the months Dad was gone, I became my mother's confidant. She told me everything. When I realized I had seen and heard much more than a seventeen-year-old boy should know, it was too late. I decided never to forgive my father for hurting my mother so deeply and for making my childhood such a crazy mess. Six months after Mom kicked him out, he moved back in. For good.

Since then, twelve years ago, Dad and I have kept our distance. We've seen each other regularly, but have never really moved beyond pleasant conversation. Over the past year, however, my sometimes funny, ever-entertaining father has been consistently warm and charming. And I find myself both heartened and bewildered in his company, wondering if I might some day share with him the thoughts and feelings I've never been able to.

These days, Dad wants to know who I'm dating, how work is going, what I think of the world around me. I'm on the brink of letting him into my life, but doing so scares me to death. When I hesitate before sharing anything important, I feel like the seventeen-year-old boy with the elephantine memory and the ice-cold heart, unable to forgive. But when I think about relaxing that resolve I made thirteen years ago and inviting Dad in, I realize that I'm not quite ready. I'm happy that the resolve I made so many years ago is weakening, but I also know that forgiveness takes a long, long time.

THINKING AND TALKING

Work with a partner to answer these questions about "Forgiving Dad."

1. What is a "house on fire"?

_____

_____

_____

2. What is the writer's "house on fire"?

_____

_____

_____

3. Why does he want to write about his "house on fire" now?

_____

_____

_____

4. What question is the writer trying to answer?

_____

_____

_____

5. What do you think the writer should do? Why?

_____

_____

_____

PLANNING

Now think about your own "house on fire." Choose a problem from the past that you are comfortable writing about. Answer these questions to help you plan your writing.

House on Fire Planning Guide

1. What was the problem, and when did it start? How did it start?

   _____

   _____

   _____

2. What was your reaction? Why?

   _____

   _____

   _____

3. Describe a specific event or reaction that demonstrates how difficult this was for you.

   _____

   _____

   _____

4. What did people around you say?

   _____

   _____

   _____

5. What did you say or think?

   _____

   _____

   _____

6. If the problem was resolved, how did it end? If it is still a problem, what are you asking yourself now?

   _____

   _____

   _____

> ### *Writing Prompt: House on Fire—A Struggle from My Past*
>
> Write about a time in your past when you struggled over a person or situation. Describe the situation and the people who were involved. Write about how you felt and what you said or did. Write about how the problem was solved or the questions that remain. Use descriptive details, dialogue, specific vocabulary, and interior monologue to re-create for the reader the struggle you experienced.

REVISING AND EDITING

After writing, review this checklist and make necessary changes.

- ☐ Did you begin by describing the situation and what led up to the problem?
- ☐ Did you include specific details about when, where, and why this took place?
- ☐ Did you describe who was there?
- ☐ Did you include interior monologue (what you were thinking)?
- ☐ Did you write about your feelings?
- ☐ Did you show what happened at the end?
- ☐ Did you organize the events of your story into paragraphs?
- ☐ Check your punctuation. Did you use capital letters, commas, periods, and quotation marks where they belong?
- ☐ Did you add a title to give the reader a preview of the incident?

SELF-ASSESSMENT

Congratulations on completing this process. How would you score this piece of writing?

☐ (4) Commendable   ☐ (3) Proficient   ☐ (2) Nearly Proficient   ☐ (1) Developing

Scoring Guide for Lesson 5: House on Fire

GENRE: PERSONAL NARRATION

> ### *Five Features in Personal Narrative Writing*
> - Event: Narrative Description and Elaboration
> - Organization of Ideas
> - Writer's Voice
> - Language: Sentences and Vocabulary
> - Mechanics: Spelling and Grammar

4 • COMMENDABLE
- Event or situation is vividly described; includes elaboration through description, use of images, anecdotes, and specific details that enable the reader to experience the event.
- Beginning is engaging and parts of the event are presented in a clever or unusual way.
- Writer is engaged in telling the story for the reader; details are convincing; writer's personality emerges from the writing through interior monologue, dialogue, description of thoughts or feelings, or directly addressing the reader.
- Language is precise and lively. Sentences are varied and vocabulary is specific.
- Writing shows clear control of writing conventions; errors do not cause confusion.

3 • PROFICIENT
- Event is described in some detail though the reader may have questions.
- Narrative has a beginning, middle, and conclusion.
- Writer's personality comes through in writing.
- Language is clear; sentence types are varied; vocabulary is general.
- Writing shows control of writing conventions; errors do not interfere with meaning.

2 • NEARLY PROFICIENT
- Event is described incompletely or writing describes more than one event.
- Description of event moves too fast; middle or conclusion may be abrupt or missing.
- Connection between event and writer may not be clear.
- Language is simple; sentence types are mostly the same; vocabulary is limited.
- Writing does not always show control of conventions; errors may interfere with meaning.

1 • DEVELOPING
- Event is identified but may be vague, incomplete, or a list without examples.
- Organization is not clear; parts of beginning, middle, or end may be missing.
- Writing does not communicate meaning or significance of event for writer.
- Language is general and vague; sentences may be incomplete or run-on.
- Errors may interfere with meaning.

A Personal Hero

Heroes inspire us and show us what's possible. We can find heroes in history, in public life, and in our daily lives. This lesson is designed to give you an opportunity to think and write about someone you consider a hero.

GETTING STARTED

To begin, think about people you admire. They can be people you've seen, heard, read about, or know. To help you, the box lists several different categories where you may find heroes. Make a quick list of their names in the space below. Share your list with a classmate. Remember: the people you list don't have to be famous.

Sports	Music	TV/Movies	History	Your Life
•	•	•	•	•
•	•	•	•	•

Select two or three people from your list that you might like to write about. Write their names and what you consider to be their most admirable qualities:

Name	Admirable Qualities
•	
•	
•	

Now read this article about Barry Bonds from the *Houston Chronicle*. Newspaper writer Richard Justice claims that Barry Bonds is a hero for two reasons. As you read, look for the two reasons and answers to these questions. Highlight the answers when you find them.

1. According to the writer, what are Bonds's admirable qualities?

2. What do others say about Bonds?

3. What specific details does the writer include to show Bonds's admirable qualities?

4. To which other player does the writer compare Bonds?

Bonds Is a Double Hero

By Richard Justice, *Houston Chronicle*

The problem with Barry Bonds is that we've come to accept his greatness as the norm. He's so much better than any other player that, in the end, he can only be compared to himself. So this year is no big deal. He has had seasons when he has hit more home runs, driven in more runs and hit for a higher batting average. He has been such an average Barry that Albert Pujols may be voted the National League's Most Valuable Player. Bonds already has five MVP trophies, which is two more than any other player in history, so what's wrong with spreading the trophies around? Except for one thing. He's still the best player in the game, and even in an average (for him) season, he's still doing spectacular things. And he has done them while watching cancer ravage his father, Bobby Bonds, who died Saturday.

"There has got to be a league somewhere on another planet where he could be an average guy," Giants manager Felipe Alou said. Bonds leads the National League in home runs, slugging percentage, on-base percentage and walks. He's third in batting average, and because he gets so few pitches to hit, is 16th with 79 RBIs. Pujols probably will win because he has been better in some of the more basic measuring-stick statistics. He leads the National League with a .365 batting average (Bonds is third at .339), is second with 108 RBIs and tied for third with 34 home runs. Pujols may hit the ball harder more consistently than any man on earth, including Bonds. Yet at 39, Bonds is as good as ever.

He left the Giants last weekend to be with his father. He returned and, in two of his first three games back, hit a pair of moon-shot, walk-off home runs to defeat the Braves. "It's such a credit to him and his mental game to be able to focus like that," Giants reliever Tim Worrell said. "I'm glad I'm on his team." Bonds called a team meeting before Tuesday's game. "He talked to all of us to explain how things are and how he feels and everything and how he's going to try to help the team amidst all the sadness and sleepless nights," Alou said. On Tuesday, Braves manager Bobby Cox headed for the clubhouse the moment Bonds swung the bat. "I just picked up my stuff to go home," Cox said. "It's a different sound. He hits the ball harder on a line than anybody I've ever seen."

Cox and Braves pitching coach Leo Mazzone had emphasized before the series that their pitchers were not to throw Bonds a pitch in the strike zone in important situations. Then Ray King did it on Tuesday, and Trey Hodges did it on Thursday. "We have a plan not to pitch Bonds in any situation like this," Cox said. "I don't know what happened to the pitch. Maybe I should have gone out and reinforced the plan."

Bonds has six home runs this month, and with 652 for his career, he needs eight more to tie his godfather, Willie Mays, for third place on the all-time list. When Bonds catches Mays, only Hank Aaron (775) and Babe Ruth (714) will be in front of him. After Thursday's game-winner, teammate Jose Cruz Jr. said, "It's all part of the movie. The guy is just amazing. He really is."

Bonds has seldom offered much of himself for public consumption, but this week he let his guard down a bit. "My dad wants everybody to know that he thanks them for all their support and prayers—especially all the baseball players that he played with," Bonds said. When he homered Tuesday night, Bonds stood at home plate and pointed skyward as the ball sailed out of the park. He sent word to the Braves that he wasn't showboating. "I owe the Braves an apology. I hope they understand," he said. "I've just got a lot of emotion. The early celebration like that, I hope they don't take offense to it. I hope no one is offended by the early celebration of my home run. I just had a lot of emotions going through me for my dad."

THINKING AND TALKING

After reading, work with a partner to complete the following chart by writing notes from the reading selection.

1. Who is the hero the writer discusses?

_____

2. What are his admirable qualities?

_____

_____

_____

_____

3. Which events show these admirable qualities?

_____

_____

_____

_____

4. How does this person compare to another similar person?

_____

_____

_____

5. What do others say about this personal hero (and how do they also show these admirable qualities)?

_____

_____

_____

6. What's your opinion about the writer's personal hero?

_____

_____

_____

PLANNING

Now choose the personal hero you want to write about. Use the same questions to gather and organize information about your hero. When you write, you can follow the order of ideas in this Planning Guide, or you can change the order. Use your own paper if you need more space.

A Personal Hero Planning Guide	
What's the name of your personal hero? When did you first learn about or discover or meet this person?	
Introduce the reader to your personal hero by adding some basic information that shows why you admire this person.	
What are your personal hero's admirable qualities?	
Which specific details show these admirable qualities?	
How does this person compare to another similar person?	
What do others say about this person (and how do they also show these admirable qualities)?	
What else can you say or show about your personal hero?	

> **_Writing Prompt: A Personal Hero_**
>
> Write about someone you admire. This person can be someone close to you, such as a family member, a friend, an acquaintance, or someone you don't know but know a lot about. Use what you have read and discussed and written already to write an essay that presents and supports the admirable qualities your personal hero exhibits.

REVISING AND EDITING

After writing, review this checklist and make necessary changes.

- ☐ Did you begin by introducing your personal hero, saying how you know (or know about) this person and why he or she is admirable?
- ☐ Did you include specific details that enable the reader to meet your personal hero?
- ☐ Did you write about your personal hero in a way that shows how you feel and why you chose to write about this person?
- ☐ Did you describe a particular incident that shows why this person is admirable?
- ☐ Did you include testimonials (what others say or have said) about your hero or interior monologue that reveals how you think or feel about this person?
- ☐ Did you organize your writing into an engaging beginning, a middle that develops a description of your personal hero, and an ending that ties everything together?
- ☐ Did you organize your main sections of your essay into paragraphs?
- ☐ Did you use language that is specific?
- ☐ Did you vary your sentence types?
- ☐ Check your punctuation. Did you use capital letters, commas, periods, and quotation marks where they belong?
- ☐ Did you title your essay?

SELF-ASSESSMENT

Congratulations on completing this process. How would you score this piece of writing?

☐ (4) Commendable   ☐ (3) Proficient   ☐ (2) Nearly Proficient   ☐ (1) Developing

Scoring Guide for Lesson 6: A Personal Hero

GENRE: FOCUSED BIOGRAPHY

> ### *Five Features in Focused Biography Writing*
> - Characterization: Description of the Person
> - Organization of Ideas
> - Writer's Voice
> - Language: Sentences and Vocabulary
> - Mechanics: Spelling and Grammar

---

4 • COMMENDABLE
- Portrays a person clearly and effectively; includes a variety of descriptive strategies such as use of images, anecdotes, and specific details to enable the reader to meet the personal hero.
- Beginning engages reader, middle develops ideas, and conclusion fits; ideas may be presented in a clever or unusual way.
- The writer's personality emerges from the writing through interior monologue, dialogue, description of thoughts or feelings, or directly addressing the reader.
- Language is generally precise and lively. Sentences are varied and vocabulary is specific.
- Writing shows clear control of writing conventions; errors do not cause confusion.

3 • PROFICIENT
- Portrays a personal hero and includes elaborative details, though the reader may have questions.
- Has a beginning, middle, and conclusion.
- Writing helps reader get to know the writer (as well as the writer's hero); significance of hero is clear.
- Language is clear; sentence types may be mostly the same; vocabulary is general.
- Writing shows control of writing conventions; errors do not interfere with meaning.

2 • NEARLY PROFICIENT
- Describes a person incompletely or presents more than one personal hero; the descriptive details may not be convincing.
- Person is introduced, but piece moves too fast; conclusion may be abrupt or missing.
- Writing does not capture personality or attitude of writer; examples may seem unbelievable.
- Language is simple; sentence types are mostly the same; vocabulary is limited.
- Errors may be distracting.

1 • DEVELOPING
- Personal hero is identified but description is a list without examples or is vague or incomplete.
- Organization is not clear; parts of beginning, middle, end may be abrupt or missing.
- Writing does not communicate meaning or significance of personal hero.
- Language is general and vague; there may be incomplete or run-on sentences.
- Errors may make it difficult for reader to understand ideas.

Lucky Breaks

Sometimes it feels as if no one else has it as bad as we do, but the truth is that we all face challenges. We can experience bad luck, loss, and hardship at any point in our lives. Some believe that hardship teaches people to be strong and work hard. Do you agree?

Often during difficult times, we come across *lucky breaks,* people or events that change our situation from bad to good. These lucky breaks can be specific people who assist us, advise us, or support us away from the difficulty. Lucky breaks can also be a random turn of events, simply good luck that moves us out of misery. Sometimes a huge event can precipitate a change, and sometimes a very small break—one that others don't even notice.

Here's your opportunity to write about a person or event that turned the tide or had a positive influence on you or someone you know. The focus of this writing is on the lucky break, the person or event that changed a situation, but you'll need to include details about what the situation was before and after the lucky break.

GETTING STARTED

To begin, think of a few lucky breaks you've experienced or observed. Jot down notes about these in the space below.

Lucky Breaks I've Experienced or Observed

The Lucky Break	What Was True BEFORE	What Was True AFTER
1.		
2.		
3.		

READING

Read this excerpt from "Life Lessons." In this selection, Adela Acosta writes about both people and events that changed the course of her life. These lucky breaks helped her develop the skills she depends on in her career. As you read, underline the people and events that were the writer's lucky breaks.

Life Lessons

By Adela Acosta

My family arrived from Puerto Rico with the dreams that permeate immigrant thinking. I was six years old, young and naïve, when I entered a public school in Harlem. English, a new language to me, sounded like rocks dropping into a river. My teachers thought that if they spoke in a very loud voice I would understand what they were saying. One called me stupid. I decided to keep quiet. In order to survive that first year, I colored. I often brag that I can out-color any kindergartner in the nation.

A social worker discovered my plight and advised me to change schools. My family sent me to St. Paul's parochial school in the heart of Spanish Harlem. There were other children like me at this school. At St. Paul's, I met Miss Mary Sheehan, a young teacher recently arrived from Dublin. She had dedicated her life to helping poor immigrant children and proceeded to lead us on a journey of self-discovery. She told me that reading was my way out—a direct accessible path to anywhere I decided to go. I began to read all the time. Eventually, I could read long books and found they gave me comfort and provided an escape from my difficult living situation.

In addition, my grandmother gave me hope and unconditional love. I was the medium for her interaction with the English-speaking world; she was my inspiration for becoming a teacher. I was teaching my family all the time. I would read to my grandmother in English, and she would teach me how to read in Spanish. Abuelita gave me optimism, courage, love and determination.

After high school and attempts at positions that didn't work for me, I realized that I was intended to become a teacher. I completed my undergraduate degree in secondary education and went on to obtain my master's degree. I am currently a principal at Cesar Chavez Elementary School in Maryland. Recently I began my doctoral studies in educational leadership.

I know now I was born to be a teacher. My turbulent upbringing and the challenges that I faced as a young person prepared me for my true vocation. My early experiences in school, the isolation I felt from my friends, the ways in which my family depended on me, and the inspiration from my grandmother helped me become what I am today.

THINKING AND TALKING

1. Work with a partner to complete the following graphic organizer about Acosta's "lucky breaks."

BEFORE: What the writer's life was like

- How she felt

- What others said or did

- What she did

LUCKY BREAKS: People or events that changed the situation

- Person or Event #1

- Person or Event #2

- Person or Event #3

AFTER: How the writer's life changed

- How she felt

- What others said or did

- What she did or became

---

2. Acosta uses vocabulary that helps the reader understand and imagine her situation. Go back to the reading selection and underline these words and phrases. Work with a classmate to explain what they mean:

    permeate • naïve • brag • plight • accessible path • medium • turbulent

3. Look for a comparison in Acosta's writing. Put a circle around it. Explain to a classmate what she means through the comparison.

PLANNING

Now, using the same graphic organizer as you did in the previous activity, develop details about one or more lucky breaks you've observed or experienced.

Lucky Breaks Planning Guide

---

1. What situation have you chosen?
   BEFORE: What your (or another person's) life was like

   - How you or another felt

   - What others said or did

   - What you or another did

   LUCKY BREAKS: People or events that changed the situation

   - Person or Event #1

   - Person or Event #2

   - Person or Event #3

   AFTER: How life changed

   - How you or another person felt

   - What you or another person said or did

   - What you or another did or became

2. Choose some vivid words or phrases that vividly describe your situation.

   _____

   _____

   _____

3. Write a comparison to help the reader imagine what happened and how you (or the person you're writing about) felt.

   _____

   _____

   _____

> ### *Writing Prompt: Lucky Breaks*
>
> Write about a situation where you've experienced or observed one or more lucky breaks. You can write about your own lucky breaks or another's good luck. Explain what the situation was before and after the lucky break, be sure to give the reader lots of details about what happened to change the tide, and show the reader the results of that change.

REVISING AND EDITING

After writing, review this checklist and make necessary changes.

- ☐ Did you begin by capturing your reader's interest with a description of the early situation?
- ☐ Did you include specific details about when and where and why this took place?
- ☐ Did you describe who was there?
- ☐ Did you include interior monologue (what you were thinking)?
- ☐ Did you show what or who intervened to change things?
- ☐ Did you show what changed?
- ☐ Did you use vivid vocabulary—words or expressions to help the reader imagine what it was like for you?
- ☐ Did you include one or more comparisons to dramatize your situation?
- ☐ Did you organize the descriptions and events into paragraphs?
- ☐ Check your punctuation. Did you use capital letters, commas, periods, and quotation marks where they belong?
- ☐ Did you add a title to give the reader a hint about your topic and make the piece inviting?

SELF-ASSESSMENT

Congratulations on completing this process. How would you score this piece of writing?

☐ (4) Commendable   ☐ (3) Proficient   ☐ (2) Nearly Proficient   ☐ (1) Developing

Scoring Guide for Lesson 7: Lucky Breaks

GENRE: NARRATIVE WRITING

> ### *Five Features in Narrative Writing*
> - Presentation and Development of the Lucky Breaks
> - Organization of Ideas: Before and After
> - Writer's Voice
> - Language: Sentences and Vocabulary
> - Mechanics: Spelling and Grammar

4 • COMMENDABLE

- Presents one or more lucky breaks and shows importance or significance through vivid and dramatic description of situation before and after; descriptive strategies such as images, anecdotes, comparisons, and specific details enable the reader to empathize with the writer.
- Beginning engages reader and establishes the "before"; middle develops lucky break and presents what changed; conclusion reveals significance of what happened.
- The writer's personality emerges from the writing through interior monologue, dialogue, description of thoughts or feelings, or by directly addressing the reader.
- Language is precise and lively; sentences are varied, and vocabulary is specific.
- Writing shows clear control of writing conventions; errors do not cause confusion.

3 • PROFICIENT

- Presents at least one lucky break and describes before and after; writing has some "showing" descriptions, though there may be mostly "telling."
- There is a clear beginning; the middle shows the lucky break and what changed; the conclusion conveys meaning of the events for the writer.
- Writing helps reader get to know the writer through direct or indirect expression of impact of events.
- Language is clear; sentence types may not be varied; vocabulary is general.
- Writing shows control of writing conventions; errors do not interfere with meaning.

2 • NEARLY PROFICIENT

- Presents one or more lucky breaks incompletely; before and after are brief or unbelievable.
- Situation is introduced, but piece moves too fast; events are unclear or undeveloped; conclusion may be abrupt or missing.
- Writing does not convey meaning of lucky breaks for writer.
- Language is basic; sentence types are mostly simple; vocabulary is limited.
- Errors may be distracting.

1 • DEVELOPING

- Lucky break is vague or incomplete; may be a list without explanation.
- Brief introduction, and limited elaboration of before and after. Conclusion may be missing.
- Writing does not reflect meaning of event for writer.
- Language is general and vague or there may be incomplete or run-on sentences.
- Errors may make it difficult for reader to understand ideas.

Responding to "Boar Out There"

Much of the writing students do in school requires reading a literature selection and responding to it. If the literature is good, you can relate to it even when the subject and characters come from a different place or a different time from ones you know much about.

This lesson presents a piece of fiction, then it asks you to respond to it.

GETTING STARTED

The story you will read describes an encounter between a girl and a wild boar. Wild boars are a kind of pig. Have you heard of them? Do you know anything about them? Begin by talking to your classmates about wild boars. Look at the picture of a wild boar in the space below and jot down in the space around the boar some facts you believe to be true about these animals.

What I Think Is True About Wild Boars

Now read "Boar Out There," a short story by Cynthia Rylant. As you read, look for answers to these questions:

1. Does Rylant's description of a wild boar remind you of any other animal?

2. Why does Jenny go into the woods?

3. Is Jenny the same at the end of the story as she is at the beginning?

Boar Out There

By Cynthia Rylant

Everyone in Glen Morgan knew there was a wild boar in the woods over by the Miller farm. The boar was out beyond the splintery rail fence and past the old black Dodge that somehow had ended up in the woods and was missing most of its parts. Jenny would hook her chin over the top rail of the fence, twirl a long green blade of grass in her teeth and whisper, "Boar out there."

And there were times she was sure she heard him. She imagined him running heavily through the trees, ignoring the sharp thorns and briars that raked his back and sprang away trembling. She thought he might have a golden horn on his terrible head. The boar would run deep into the woods, then rise up on his rear hooves, throw his head toward the stars and cry a long, clear, sure note into the air. The note would glide through the night and spear the heart of the moon. The boar had no fear of the moon, Jenny knew, as she lay in bed, listening.

One hot summer day she went to find the boar. No one in Glen Morgan had ever gone past the old black Dodge and beyond, as far as she knew. But the boar was there somewhere, between those awful trees, and his dark green eyes waited for someone.

Jenny felt it was she.

Moving slowly over damp brown leaves, Jenny could sense her ears tingle and fan out as she listened for thick breathing from the trees. She stopped to pick a teaberry leaf to chew, stood a minute, then went on.

Deep in the woods she kept her eyes to the sky. She needed to be reminded that there was a world above and apart from the trees—a world of space and air, air that didn't linger all about her, didn't press deep into her skin, as forest air did. Finally, leaning against a tree to rest, she heard him for the first time. She forgot to breathe, standing there listening to the stamping of hooves, and she choked and coughed. Coughed!

And now the pounding was horrible, too loud and confusing for Jenny. Horrible. She stood stiff with wet eyes and knew she could always pray, but for some reason didn't. He came through the trees so fast that she had no time to scream or run. And he was there before her. His large gray-black body shivered as he waited just beyond the shadow of the tree she held for support. His nostrils glistened, and his eyes; but astonishingly, he was silent. He shivered and glistened and was absolutely silent.

Jenny matched his silence, and her body was rigid, but not her eyes. They traveled along his scarred, bristling back to his thick hind legs. Tears spilling and flooding her face, Jenny stared at the boar's ragged ears, caked with blood. Her tears dropped to the leaves, and the only sound between them was his slow breathing. Then the boar snorted and jerked. But Jenny did not move.

High in the trees a blue jay yelled, and, suddenly, it was over. Jenny stood like a rock as the boar wildly flung his head and in terror bolted past her. Past her. . . .

And now, since that summer, Jenny still hooks her chin over the old rail fence, and she still whispers, "Boar out there." But when she leans on the fence, looking into the trees, her eyes are full and she leaves wet patches on the splintery wood. She is sorry for the torn ears of the boar and sorry that he has no golden horn.

But mostly she is sorry that he lives in fear of blue jays and little girls, when every-one in Glen Morgan lives in fear of him.

THINKING, TALKING, AND PLANNING

Work with a partner to answer the following questions. You will use some of these answers in your essay, so take notes on the lines below each question.

1. What do you remember first about the story—what scene or thoughts or actions stood out for you?

_____

_____

_____

_____

_____

2. How do Jenny and the townspeople feel about the boar at the beginning of the story? What are Jenny's feelings about the boar at the end of the story?

_____

_____

_____

_____

_____

3. Were there memorable sounds, sights, or feelings in this story? What were they? What was the writer trying to emphasize by including these details?

_____

_____

_____

_____

_____

4. What did Jenny learn? Have you ever had a similar experience in which you learned something unexpected? What happened?

_____

_____

_____

_____

_____

5. There are several ideas in the story. Which are some of the important ideas? Look at all the ideas first, then decide which are important ones and which are not important. Look for at least five important ideas and check them. When you are finished, talk with a partner about which ideas you think are important and why.

☐ a. Jenny imagined that the boar was strong and powerful.

☐ b. The old black Dodge was missing most of its parts.

☐ c. The boar was fearful of most everything.

☐ d. The boar moved fast.

☐ e. Jenny was the first person to go into the woods to search for the boar.

☐ f. The boar's nostrils and eyes glistened.

☐ g. Jenny imagined the boar to be different from what it was.

☐ h. It is very hot and humid during the summer in Glen Morgan.

☐ i. Jenny is disappointed that her dream of the boar is not real.

6. Which image or images from the selection were powerful for you? Choose one, write it down, and tell why you think it was powerful or important.

_____

_____

_____

_____

_____

7. Compare an important idea in "Boar Out There" to an important idea from something else you've read, watched on TV, or seen in a film. Show how two writers or directors have worked with similar ideas.

_____

_____

_____

_____

_____

_____

> ### *Writing Prompt: Response to Literature*
>
> Write an essay in response to "Boar Out There." Choose one of the following topics. Use your notes from any of the preceding sections to develop and support the ideas in your essay.
>
> - Topic 1: In your opinion, what was an important idea communicated in this story? What was the writer trying to show? Be detailed, and use language from the story to support your opinion.
> - Topic 2: How does an important idea from the story connect with your life or the life of someone you know? Present an important idea that relates to that personal experience or relationship.
> - Topic 3: Choose an important idea in "Boar Out There" and compare it to a theme or idea from something else you've read or seen on TV or in a movie. Show how two writers or directors have handled similar ideas.

REVISING AND EDITING

After writing, review this checklist and make necessary changes.

- ☐ Did you begin in an interesting way that leads to the purpose of your essay?

- ☐ Did you identify the story and the author?

- ☐ Did you early in your essay state its point—that is, the main idea (your interpretation, the connection, a comparison and the use of an image) of your essay?

- ☐ Did you support your main idea by including specific references to the text, specific examples, and explanations that show how your interpretation makes sense?

- ☐ Did you show in your writing that you have thoroughly understood the text?

- ☐ Did you organize the main sections of your essay into paragraphs so that the reader can follow your ideas?

- ☐ Check your punctuation. Did you use capital letters, commas, periods, and quotation marks where they belong?

- ☐ How about the ending? Did you end with a confident conclusion that restates your main point?

- ☐ Did you title your essay?

SELF-ASSESSMENT

Congratulations on completing this process. How would you score this piece of writing?

☐ (4) Commendable   ☐ (3) Proficient   ☐ (2) Nearly Proficient   ☐ (1) Developing

Scoring Guide for Lesson 8: Responding to "Boar Out There"

GENRE: RESPONSE TO LITERATURE

> ### *Five Features in Response to Literature Writing*
> - Interpretation: What the Reading Selection Means to the Writer
> - Organization of Ideas and Support for Interpretation
> - Voice: Writer's Point of View
> - Language: Sentences and Vocabulary
> - Mechanics: Spelling and Grammar

4 • COMMENDABLE
- Interpretation is well developed, perceptive, and convincing to the reader; quotes, paraphrases, comparisons demonstrate understanding.
- Interpretation is organized with an engaging beginning, elaborated middle, and summary ending around specific ideas, events, or images; convincing support expands and deepens response.
- Writer's point of view is presented in an appropriate way; reader awareness is evident.
- Language is vivid and lively; sentences are varied and vocabulary is specific.
- Writing shows mastery of writing conventions; errors do not cause confusion.

3 • PROFICIENT
- Presents a clear interpretation that recognizes one or more important ideas; writing refers to specific quotes or passages in text.
- Interpretation is organized through one or more ideas; claims are supported through relevant evidence.
- Writer's opinion or attitude may be included.
- Language is clear; sentence types are varied; vocabulary may be general.
- Errors do not interfere with meaning.

2 • NEARLY PROFICIENT
- Presents a response that may be linked to text but does not make a convincing connection to the reading.
- Interpretation may not be organized around ideas; writing may not include relevant evidence and may not be convincing.
- Writer's point of view may dominate or may be missing altogether.
- Language is simple; sentence types are mostly the same; vocabulary may be limited.
- Errors may be distracting.

1 • DEVELOPING
- Response may be linked to text but is unclear or incomplete.
- Organization is unclear; support for interpretation is brief, incomplete, or not convincing.
- Response may be entirely point of view and no interpretation.
- Language is general and vague and there may be incomplete or run-on sentences.
- Errors may make it difficult for reader to understand writer's ideas.

Responding to "The Cormorant's Tale"

Gwendolyn Brooks, a well-known poet who spoke out about taboo topics, has said that poetry is "life distilled." That is, poems can describe the barest, most essential elements of human experience. We can learn a lot, then, by reading and responding to poetry. This lesson will give you an opportunity to read a poem and write about what the poem means to you.

GETTING STARTED

In certain parts of the world, people use birds to catch fish. These birds are called cormorants, and they are very skillful at spotting and snatching fish. Though they might like to eat the fish they catch, they cannot because the fishermen put rings around their necks to prevent them from swallowing. What do you think of this method of catching fish? Do you think it is clever? Unkind? What do you think a bird catching a fish looks like? Draw a picture of a fisherman and a cormorant catching a fish. Then talk to a classmate about your ideas and your drawing.

Drawing: Fishing with a Bird

READING

Before you read "The Cormorant's Tale," answer these questions by talking to a classmate:

1. If you were a cormorant, how would you feel about your job to catch fish?

2. What words or images do you expect to see in the poem? (Images are words that help us see pictures in our minds.)

3. After reading the title of the poem, from whose point of view do you think the poem is written?

Read the poem with your partner. One of you will read the left side and the other will read the right side. Sometimes you'll read at the same time. Your teacher may ask you to perform your reading for the class.

The Cormorant's Tale

By Paul Fleischman

"As free as a bird"	"As free as a bird"
	I've heard my man say
And I choke when I hear it	Consider my case.
I'm an old cormorant	I'm an old cormorant
That's my man	
with the rope	Attached to the ring
That circles my throat.	
Like all cormorants	Like all cormorants
	At catching fish I excel
The skill's in my bones	As my owner knows well.
It's a cormorant's life	It's a cormorant's life
To dive down—as right now.	
	I spot a fish and I seize it
I'm a practiced sea-fowl.	
But I'm a caught cormorant	But I'm a caught cormorant
	—Not the first nor the last—
And the rings	
round our necks	Stop us eating our catch.
Just to taste is our fate	Just to taste is our fate
Though our stomachs are sore	
	But they take the fish
Then we dive after more.	
I'm a cormorant, yes	I'm a cormorant, yes
	And I'll tell you my wish:
To be free and unfettered—	
As free as a fish.	As free as a fish.

112   Prompted to Write

THINKING, TALKING, AND PLANNING

Work with a partner to complete the following activities.

1. Go back to your drawing from the "Getting Started" section and change or add details so that the drawing includes details from the poem.

2. The poem is written from the cormorant's point of view. With your partner, jot below three statements that the cormorant would say or believe based on what you read in the poem.

3. Now imagine the points of view of the fisherman and the fish. Fill in the "talk bubbles" with something they would say or believe.

4. With your partner, talk about one or more images you found in the poem. What do they represent or make you think about? Do the combined images suggest a theme, or bigger idea, in the poem? Use the chart below to record your ideas.

Images		
What the images represent		
Themes		

5. Now jot down an important idea from "The Cormorant's Tale"—something that you think the poet was trying to communicate in the cormorant's voice.

_____

_____

_____

_____

_____

> ### *Writing Prompt: Response to a Poem*
>
> Write an essay in response to "The Cormorant's Tale." Choose one of the following topics. Use your notes from preceding sections to develop your essay.
>
> - Topic 1: Reread "The Cormorant's Tale" to yourself. What overall idea, or theme, was the writer communicating? Did the writer succeed? If so, how did he succeed: what tricks and devices did he use to get to his success? Did he fail? Why exactly did he fail? Be specific in your essay.
> - Topic 2: How does an important idea from "The Cormorant's Tale" connect to you or to someone you know? Present an important idea that relates to a personal experience or relationship. Write about a related situation, and show how it connects to the poem.
> - Topic 3: Choose an important idea in the poem and compare it to a theme or idea from something else you've read or seen on TV or in a film. Show how two writers or directors (Fleischman and someone else) have handled similar topics.

REVISING AND EDITING

After writing, review this checklist and make necessary changes.

- ☐ Did you begin in an interesting way that leads to the purpose of your essay?
- ☐ Did you name the poem and the poet?
- ☐ Did you state the main idea (your interpretation, your evaluation, a connection, a comparison, or the use of an image) of your essay?
- ☐ Did you support your main idea by including references to the poem, specific examples, and explanations that persuade the reader that your interpretation makes sense?
- ☐ Did you explain what the poem means to you?
- ☐ Did you organize the main sections of your essay into paragraphs?
- ☐ Check your punctuation. Did you use capital letters, commas, periods, and quotation marks where they belong?
- ☐ Did you end with a confident conclusion that restates your purpose?
- ☐ Did you title your essay?

SELF-ASSESSMENT

Congratulations on completing this process. How would you score this piece of writing?

☐ (4) Commendable ☐ (3) Proficient ☐ (2) Nearly Proficient ☐ (1) Developing

Scoring Guide for Lesson 9: Responding to "The Cormorant's Tale"

GENRE: RESPONSE TO POETRY

Five Features in Response to Poetry
- Interpretation: What the Poem Means to the Writer
- Organization of Ideas and Support for Interpretation
- Voice: Writer's Point of View
- Language: Sentences and Vocabulary
- Mechanics: Spelling and Grammar

---

4 • COMMENDABLE
- Interpretation is well developed and perceptive and demonstrates a thorough understanding of the poem; quotes or other details are referenced.
- Interpretation is organized around specific ideas or images and is convincingly supported through specific and relevant references to the poem.
- Writer's point of view is presented in an appropriate way; reader awareness is evident.
- Language is precise and lively; sentences are varied; and vocabulary is specific.
- Writing shows clear control of writing conventions; errors do not cause confusion.

3 • PROFICIENT
- Presents a clear interpretation that recognizes one or more important ideas; refers to specific words or lines to explain meaning.
- Interpretation is organized through one or more ideas; interpretation is supported through relevant evidence.
- Writer's opinion and attitude may be included.
- Language is clear; sentence types are varied; vocabulary is general.
- Errors do not interfere with meaning.

2 • NEARLY PROFICIENT
- Interpretation is linked to the poem but does not demonstrate a thorough reading.
- Interpretation may not be organized around ideas; interpretation may not include relevant evidence and may not be convincing.
- Writer's point of view may dominate or may be missing altogether.
- Language is simple; sentence types are simple or mostly the same; vocabulary is limited.
- Errors may be distracting.

1 • DEVELOPING
- Interpretation may be linked to the poem but is unclear or incomplete.
- Organization is unclear; support for interpretation is brief or incomplete and is not convincing.
- Response may be entirely point of view and no interpretation.
- Language is general and vague; sentences may be incomplete or run-on.
- Errors may interfere with meaning.

lesson
10

Here's Something Cool!

Every day it seems new products appear. Electronic gadgets, cell phones, computers, and automobiles are constantly being updated and improved. Consumers have a hard time keeping up with all that's new. Young people know a lot about what's new. Here's your chance to identify a product or a service you think is cool and present it to a general audience.

GETTING STARTED

To begin, work with a classmate to make a list of five terrific products or services popular with consumers. Try to think of things that improve life for lots of people, rather than simply being fancier or more convenient.

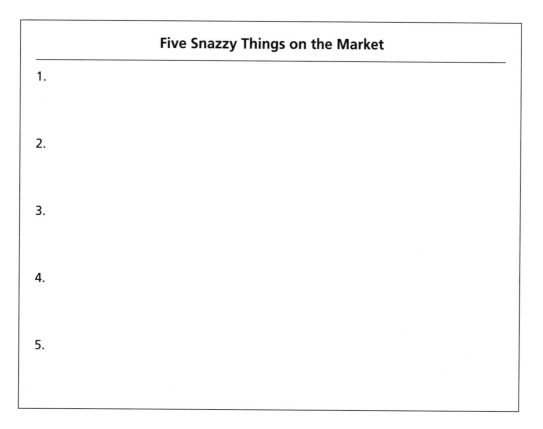

Five Snazzy Things on the Market

1.

2.

3.

4.

5.

READING

Read "Never Miss Anything Again on Television." This article appeared in a newspaper column called "Cutting Edge," a regular feature that introduces new products and services. While you read, code the article by writing:

1 = Where the writer explains what the product is

2 = Where the writer describes how the product works

3 = Where the writer matches the product to a particular group or type of person

4 = Where the writer adds some special features

5 = Where the writer relates a personal experience with the product

Never Miss Anything Again on Television
From "Cutting Edge" (*Marin Independent Journal*)

Even the most devoted couch potato can't watch television all the time. But tveye.com can. This Web-based service bills itself as a search engine for TV and radio. It scans the closed captions that accompany most television programming for keywords selected by users.

For audio broadcasts, it employs a special speech-to-text program that quickly produces searchable text. Soon after your keyword has been mentioned, TVEyes sends you an email message containing the reference and a link to a partial transcript. A free version of the service allows you to track up to three keywords or phrases; subscription versions (starting at $500 a month) offer features like unlimited keywords and direct access to a video or audio clip containing your keywords.

The primary subscribers are marketers, investors, government agencies and consumers. Ordinary consumers mostly use it to pursue personal interests and for celebrity watching.

Keywords typed into the Web site one recent afternoon included "monarch butterfly," "handcuffs" and "Andre Agassi." Users can limit the kinds of programming searched, thereby avoiding meaningless though perhaps amusing references. For instance, when "opera" was selected as a keyword, one of the results included banter from a "Seinfeld" rerun.

The service is seeking a partnership with a Web search engine. Ken Brachfeld of Fairfield, Conn., who uses TVEyes to follow investment and special-education-related keywords, said via email that he would "love to see TVEyes results incorporated into a Google or Yahoo results page. I'd be all over that."

"Right now our most aggressive users are political campaigners. They are constantly adding and deleting keywords as news cycles change."

THINKING AND TALKING

After reading, answer these questions with a classmate. Use your own words.

1. What is the product the article discusses?

_____

_____

_____

_____

2. What does the product do?

_____

_____

_____

_____

3. Who is the product for?

_____

_____

_____

_____

4. Would you use this product? What would you search for? Why?

_____

_____

_____

_____

_____

_____

_____

5. Now identify a cool product or service on the market that you would like to discuss with your classmates.

_____

_____

_____

_____

PLANNING

1. First jot down some notes on your product.

Note-Taking Grid for Your Product

What's your product?	How does it work?
Who should use it?	What is a special feature?
What happened when you first used it?	Why should your classmates buy it?

---

2. Now organize your ideas for your writing. When you write, use the example of the article to follow this sequence.

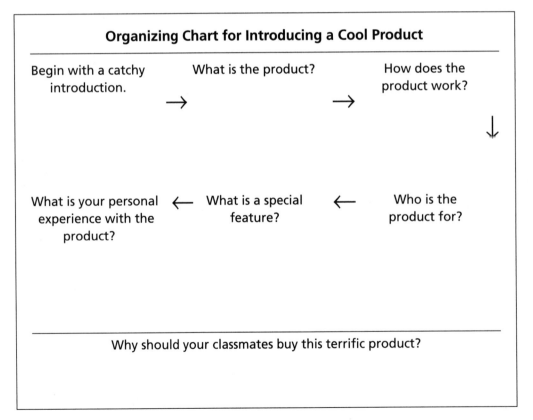

Organizing Chart for Introducing a Cool Product

Begin with a catchy introduction. → What is the product? → How does the product work? ↓

What is your personal experience with the product? ← What is a special feature? ← Who is the product for?

Why should your classmates buy this terrific product?

> ### *Writing Prompt: Here's Something Cool!*
>
> Write an essay discussing and selling a product or service. Select something that has or will have a positive impact on people's lives. Connect your product to architecture, transportation, communication, or industrial design, on any aspect of daily life.
>
> Describe the product clearly and explain how it is used. Write about special features and who might use it. Include, if possible, your personal experience with the product. Use an engaging opening and enthusiasm to be persuasive.

REVISING AND EDITING

After writing, review this checklist and make necessary changes.

- [ ] Did you begin with a catchy introduction that draws the reader in?
- [ ] Did you describe your product?
- [ ] Did you include specific details about the product?
- [ ] Did you explain how it works?
- [ ] Did you add one or more special features?
- [ ] Did you include a description of what happened when you used the product?
- [ ] Did you organize the ideas of your essay in paragraphs in an order similar to the article that is easy to follow?
- [ ] Check your punctuation. Did you use capital letters, periods, commas, and quotation marks where they belong?
- [ ] How about the ending? Did you make an enthusiastic recommendation?
- [ ] Did you add a title?

SELF-ASSESSMENT

Congratulations on completing this process. How would you score this piece of writing?

- [ ] (4) Commendable - [ ] (3) Proficient - [ ] (2) Nearly Proficient - [ ] (1) Developing

Scoring Guide for Lesson 10:
Here's Something Cool!

GENRE: INFORMATION WRITING

Five Features in Information Writing

- Clarity of Topic and Reason for Writing
- Organization of Ideas and Points of Emphasis
- Audience Awareness: Addresses Reader Questions and Concerns
- Language: Sentences and Explicit Vocabulary
- Mechanics: Spelling and Grammar

---

4 • COMMENDABLE

- Topic is clear and presented in engaging or original way; reader understands why writer has presented topic; presentation is entertaining.
- Beginning engages reader; middle deepens and develops topic by identifying important points; conclusion fits.
- Writing shows reader awareness by presenting strong arguments and convincing reasons.
- Language is persuasive, precise, and lively; sentences are varied; and vocabulary adds to the persuasiveness of the writing.
- Writing shows clear control of writing conventions, though there may be a few errors.

3 • PROFICIENT

- Topic is clearly presented and background is provided.
- Clear beginning, middle, and conclusion; important points are emphasized.
- Writing addresses reader questions and concerns.
- Language is clear; sentence types are varied; vocabulary is specific and persuasive.
- Writing shows control of writing conventions; errors do not interfere with meaning.

2 • NEARLY PROFICIENT

- Topic is introduced but it may be vague or incomplete; reader is left with many questions.
- Topic is introduced but development moves too fast; middle and conclusion may be abrupt or missing.
- Writing does not address most reader concerns.
- Language is simple; sentence types are mostly simple or the same; vocabulary is general.
- Errors may interfere with meaning.

1 • DEVELOPING

- Topic may be brief or difficult to identify; reason for selecting it is brief.
- Brief introduction (or only introduction); limited explanation; and conclusion may be missing.
- Reader awareness is not apparent.
- Language is general and vague; sentences may be incomplete or run-on.
- Errors may interfere with meaning.

Junk Food Lunches?

W hat do you eat for lunch? Do you make yourself a sandwich to bring to school, buy a slice of pizza in the cafeteria, or rely on the school vending machines? How important is it to eat nutritious food?

Some people think it's very important for students to eat healthy food. In fact, new legislation sets higher standards so that less junk food will be available. In this lesson you'll read about food and drinks of questionable nutritional value in vending machines. You'll gather and discuss information, form an opinion, then write a persuasive essay defending your point of view.

GETTING STARTED

To begin, work with a classmate and list the food and drinks you regularly consume. Sort them into healthy and unhealthy categories.

My Normal Diet		
	Food	Drinks
Healthy		
Unhealthy		

READING

Read "School Vending Machines Dispensing Junk," an article about school vending machines. As you read, look for and highlight:

1 = Statistics

2 = Quotes

3 = Persuasive language

School Vending Machines Dispensing Junk

From the Center for Science in the Public Interest

A nationwide survey of vending machines in middle schools and high schools finds that 75 percent of the drinks and 85 percent of the snacks sold are of poor nutritional value. The study, of 1,420 vending machines in 251 schools, was organized by the Center for Science in the Public Interest (CSPI) and conducted by 120 volunteers. CSPI contends that all foods sold out of vending machines, school stores, and other venues outside of the official school lunch program should make positive contributions to children's diets and health.

"It's hard enough for parents to guide their children's food choices, but it becomes virtually impossible when public schools are peddling junk food throughout the school day," said CSPI nutrition policy director Margo G. Wootan. "Many parents who send their kids off with lunch money in the morning have no clue that it can be so readily squandered on Coke, Doritos, and HoHos."

Of the drinks sold in the 13,650 vending-machine slots surveyed, 70 percent were sugary drinks such as soda, juice drinks with less than 50 percent juice, iced tea, and "sports" drinks. Of the sodas, only 14 percent were diet, and only 12 percent of the drinks available were water. Just 5 percent of drink options were milk but of those, most (57 percent) were high-fat whole or 2 percent milk.

Of the snack foods sold in the machines, candy (42 percent), chips (25 percent) and sweet baked goods (13 percent) accounted for 80 percent of the options. Of 9,723 snack slots in all the vending machines surveyed, only 26 slots contained fruits or vegetables.

While the Department of Agriculture (USDA) sets detailed standards for nutrient content and portion sizes for the official school meals, it currently has little authority to regulate foods sold outside those meals, whether in vending machines or a la carte (snack) lines in cafeterias. According to CSPI, Congress needs to give USDA more authority to regulate such foods in order to preserve the integrity of the federal school lunch program, in which the federal government invests $8.8 billion a year.

"Junk foods in school vending machines compete with, and ultimately undermine, the nutritious meals offered by the federal school lunch program," said Senator Tom Harkin (D-IA). "Congress should step in and ensure that soda, candy, chips, and cookies don't become the de facto school lunch. USDA needs to set standards for all foods sold in schools that participate in the federal school lunch program."

Despite the financial pressures on school systems that lead them to sell junk food in the first place, some schools are voluntarily setting higher nutrition standards for vending machine foods. As it happens, says CSPI, those school districts are doing well financially by doing good—they are not experiencing a drop-off in revenue by switching to healthier foods.

"Though many assume that vending machines will only be profitable if they are stocked with junk foods, we have not seen a loss in revenue by switching to healthier options," said Carolyn P. Whitehead, the health and physical education coordinator for McComb, Mississippi school district, which now sells only water and 100 percent fruit juice in vending machines. "School administrators need to know that there's no downside to supporting better nutrition in schools."

Soda and low-nutrition snack foods are a key source of excess calories in children's diets, contribute to overweight and obesity, and displace more nutritious foods. Obesity rates have doubled in children and tripled in adolescents over the last two decades. Studies show that children's soft drink intake has increased, and children who drink more soft drinks consume more calories and are more likely to be overweight than kids who drink fewer soft drinks.

"The underfunding of No Child Left Behind has forced many schools to cut gym classes and prop up Coke machines in their hallways," said Representative Lynn Woolsey (D-CA). "The legislation that Senator Harkin and I have introduced will, however, help schools improve the quality of foods sold to students. With kids spending much of their waking hours in school, schools should be on the front line of efforts to reduce obesity, overweight, and diet-related disease."

Senator Harkin and Representative Woolsey are each leading the fight in their respective chambers to give USDA more authority to set nutrition standards for foods sold in schools.

THINKING AND TALKING

Now work with a partner to answer the following questions. Questions 1–4 are about information in the article. Questions 5–7 are about persuasive strategies in the writing.

1. What is CSPI's opinion about junk food in schools? How many times do you find the opinion restated in the article?

_____

_____

_____

_____

2. According to CSPI, what should vending machine food consist of?

_____

_____

_____

_____

3. What do CSPI and Senator Tom Harkin want Congress to do?

_____

_____

_____

_____

4. What can schools do about vending machines that sell junk food?

_____

_____

_____

_____

5. What are the problems with junk food? Would the article be more persuasive if a statement of the problem appeared earlier?

_____

_____

_____

_____

6. Go back to the article and underline these words, which are used to persuade the reader to agree with CSPI. Notice how the words try to discredit the other side.

   contends • peddling • squandered • step in • ensure • de facto

_____

_____

_____

7. Where is the counterargument in the article? Put a circle around it.

PLANNING

You will write about your opinion of junk food. Plan your persuasive essay by jotting notes in the chart below.

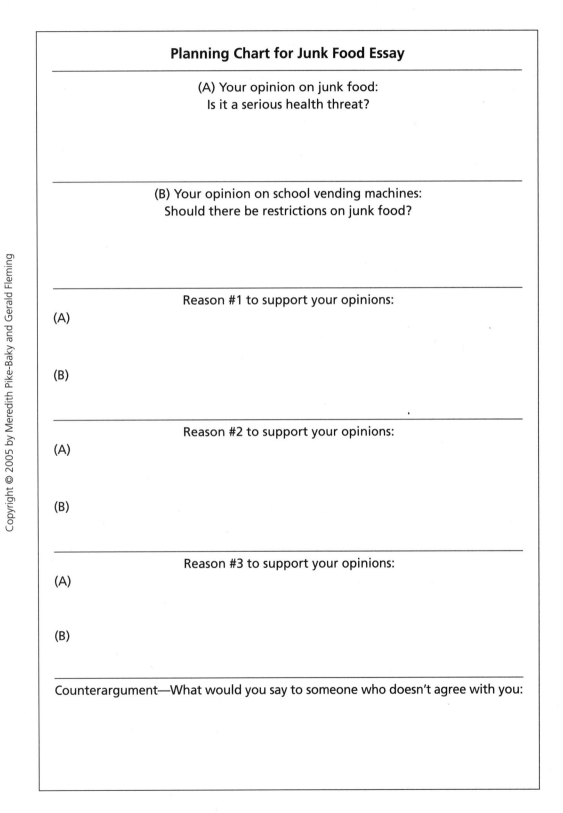

Planning Chart for Junk Food Essay

(A) Your opinion on junk food:
Is it a serious health threat?

(B) Your opinion on school vending machines:
Should there be restrictions on junk food?

Reason #1 to support your opinions:

(A)

(B)

Reason #2 to support your opinions:

(A)

(B)

Reason #3 to support your opinions:

(A)

(B)

Counterargument—What would you say to someone who doesn't agree with you:

> ### *Writing Prompt: Junk Food Lunches?*
>
> Choose one of these topics:
>
> - Topic 1: What is your opinion of raising standards for food in school vending machines?
> - Topic 2: Should junk food be banned completely from school vending machines?
>
> Write an essay stating and supporting your opinion. You will want to persuade the reader to accept your opinion, so be sure to include facts, examples, and experiences in your writing. Organize your arguments so that the reader can follow your ideas easily.

REVISING AND EDITING

After writing, review this checklist and make necessary changes.

- ☐ Did you begin with a catchy introduction that grabs the reader's interest?
- ☐ Did you explain the issue and give your opinion?
- ☐ Did you give two or three reasons to support your point of view?
- ☐ Did you use statistics, examples, or personal experiences to support your opinion?
- ☐ Did you organize your ideas into paragraphs to help the reader follow your line of thinking?
- ☐ Did you use persuasive language?
- ☐ Did you include a counterargument?
- ☐ Check your punctuation. Did you use capital letters, commas, periods, and quotation marks where they belong?
- ☐ How about the ending? Did you restate your opinion in an emphatic way?
- ☐ Did you title your essay?

SELF-ASSESSMENT

Congratulations on completing this process. How would you score this piece of writing?

☐ (4) Commendable ☐ (3) Proficient ☐ (2) Nearly Proficient ☐ (1) Developing

Scoring Guide for Lesson 11: Junk Food Lunches?

GENRE: PERSUASIVE WRITING

Five Features in Persuasive Writing

- Clarity of Position and Support of Argument
- Organization of Ideas and Focus
- Audience Awareness: Addresses Reader Questions and Concerns
- Language: Sentences and Persuasive Vocabulary
- Mechanics: Spelling and Grammar

---

4 • COMMENDABLE

- Writer's opinion is clearly stated; arguments are well supported through effective use of examples, statistics, anecdotes, or references to experts.
- Arguments are arranged and presented in an order that strengthens the persuasive power of the writing; focus points are clear and logic is easy to follow.
- Writing addresses reader concerns by presenting strong arguments and convincing reasons; may present ideas in a surprising, unusual, or entertaining way.
- Language is precise and lively; sentences are varied; and vocabulary adds to the persuasiveness of the writing.
- Writing shows clear control of writing conventions, though there may be a few errors.

3 • PROFICIENT

- Writer states opinion and supports it through one or more arguments; uses examples, statistics, anecdotes, and references to experts to persuade.
- Arguments are ordered logically and focus points are clear.
- Writing addresses reader questions and concerns.
- Language is clear; sentence types are varied; vocabulary is specific and persuasive.
- Writing shows control of writing conventions; errors do not interfere with meaning.

2 • NEARLY PROFICIENT

- Writer states opinion but it may be vague or incomplete; examples, statistics, or anecdotes do not sufficiently persuade reader.
- Order of arguments may seem random or choppy; may not focus on one or more arguments.
- Writing does not address reader concerns.
- Language is basic; sentence types are mostly simple; vocabulary is general.
- Errors may interfere with meaning.

1 • DEVELOPING

- Position may be brief or difficult to identify; support is brief.
- Organization of ideas is not clear.
- Reader awareness is not apparent.
- Language is general and vague; sentences may be incomplete or run-on.
- Errors may interfere with meaning.

Key to Success

This lesson is designed to give you an opportunity to think and talk about one or more factors that lead to success. You'll have a chance to talk to your classmates and read another's opinion. After completing the activities, your task will be presenting what you consider to be a key to success.

GETTING STARTED

To begin, think of what it means to be successful. Take some time to talk with a partner and jot down some ideas in the space below. Remember that there are lots of ways to be successful.

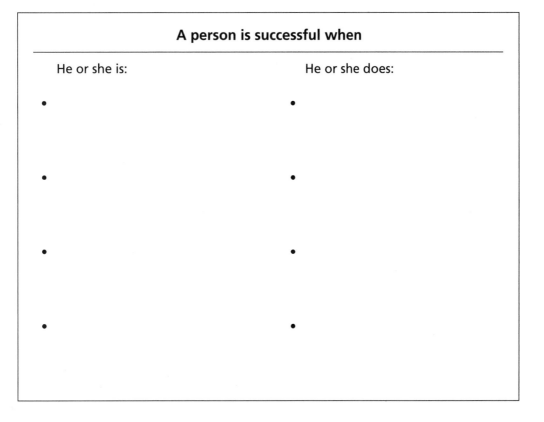

A person is successful when

He or she is:

-
-
-
-

He or she does:

-
-
-
-

READING

Now read "Education is the Key to Latino Success," an article by Mauricio Torres-Benavides. In this piece, Torres-Benavides emphasizes the importance of education in the lives of Latino students. As you read, look for how he

- Compares Latinos to another group
- Uses a well-known Latino leader to validate his opinion
- Refers to the past as well as to the future

Education is the Key to Latino Success

By Mauricio Torres-Benavides *(Marin Independent Journal)*

Si, se puede! Yes, it is possible! This has been the rallying cry for Latinos in the United States since the early 60s. At that time Cesar Chavez first organized farm workers in the fields of California to fight for their rights. Like our forefathers who first came to America, Latinos have migrated north looking for opportunities. And through arduous work and difficult living situations, they have built a distinct subculture that is now becoming part of the fabric of this nation. From farm fields to restaurants and into the business and academic centers of the future, the Latino community has struggled to succeed. Now with increased access to education, they will find success.

Chavez, a lifelong union organizer, understood that the path to Latinos' success in the U.S. was through education. He also realized that the changes in society that were necessary would take time. Indeed, the changes he wanted would take generations and they required many small successes, beginning with farm workers receiving pay for their labor. Chavez believed that "the end of all education should surely be service to others." He "walked his talk" in 1966 when he marched 340 miles from Delano to Sacramento to protest for workers' rights to organize in unions. Since that famous march, Latinos have made progress in American society, though there is still work to do.

When I speak to Latino parents of high school students in our community, two things become clear. One, parents unanimously want their kids to go to college. Secondly, they often do not understand what it takes to get them there or how to best support them. For many Latino families, the opportunity to attend college seems complicated. Fortunately, in California, students now have increased access to higher education. Students who have studied in a California high school for at least three years and have graduated can attend state colleges and universities without paying the highest fees. In addition, there are more scholarships and counseling services open to Latino students who need financial support and guidance in understanding the many steps in getting into college.

Through education, Latinos are poised for success. Programs that prepare students for technical professions, health services and teaching are plentiful. Community colleges offer the option of transferring to a larger university after two years of completed study. Education will make dreams possible. As we look to the future, we need to repeat the message that going to college and getting a certificate or a degree is not beyond the reach of young Latinos who want to be successful. Together we continue to say "Si, se puede!"

THINKING AND TALKING

After reading, work with a partner to answer these questions.

1. To which other group does the writer compare Latino immigrants?

_____

_____

2. What did Cesar Chavez do to show his beliefs?

_____

_____

_____

_____

3. What is one obstacle that blocks some Latino students from going to college?

_____

_____

_____

_____

4. How does the writer suggest Latinos overcome this obstacle?

_____

_____

_____

_____

5. Now "bring it home" and apply this to your situation. What are some other "keys to success" that you and your classmates can suggest to promote an individual's success or a group's success?

_____

_____

_____

_____

_____

_____

PLANNING

Use the structure and strategies that Torres-Benavides uses in "Education is the Key to Latino Success" to help you develop your ideas on the topic of success. Fill out the following chart.

Key to Success Planning Chart

1. In your opinion, what leads to success? Is this true for all people or, like Torres-Benavides, do you want to narrow your definition to a specific group?

2. Identify a well-known person who probably agrees with you about what leads to success. Describe this person briefly and give an example of what he or she did or said to convince others of this opinion.

3. What is at least one obstacle that prevents success? Describe the obstacle and write about how people can overcome it.

4. If people follow your advice, what does their future look like? Predict what will happen when people use the key to success that you recommend.

5. Notice how Torres-Benavides begins and ends the article with the same expression that represents and further supports his opinion. Think of a saying or proverb or quote to introduce and conclude your writing.

> ### *Writing Prompt: Key to Success*
>
> Write a speech in which you present what you consider to be the key (or keys) to success, and why this is so. Use quotes, others' experiences, and persuasive language to make your speech both entertaining and convincing.

REVISING AND EDITING

After writing, review this checklist and make necessary changes.

- ☐ Did you begin with a catchy introduction that grabs the listener's attention?
- ☐ Did you give an example of an individual or group that has shown how your key to success really works?
- ☐ Did you write about possible obstacles to success and how someone can overcome them?
- ☐ How about the ending? Did you predict what future lies ahead if people follow your key to success?
- ☐ Did you use persuasive language?
- ☐ Did you organize the main ideas of your speech into paragraphs?
- ☐ Check your punctuation. Did you use capital letters, commas, periods, and quotation marks where they belong?
- ☐ Did you title your speech?

SELF-ASSESSMENT

Congratulations on completing this process. How would you score this piece of writing?

☐ (4) Commendable   ☐ (3) Proficient   ☐ (2) Nearly Proficient   ☐ (1) Developing

Scoring Guide for Lesson 12: Key to Success

GENRE: PERSUASIVE WRITING

Five Features in Persuasive Writing

- Clarity of Position and Support of Argument
- Organization of Ideas and Focus
- Audience Awareness: Addresses Reader Questions and Concerns
- Language: Sentences and Persuasive Vocabulary
- Mechanics: Spelling and Grammar

---

4 • COMMENDABLE

- Writer's opinion is clearly stated; arguments are well supported through effective use of examples, statistics, anecdotes, or references to experts.
- Arguments are arranged and presented in an order that strengthens the persuasive power of the writing; focus points are clear; and logic is easy to follow.
- Writing addresses reader or listener concerns by presenting strong arguments and convincing reasons; may present ideas in a surprising, unusual, or entertaining way.
- Language is precise and lively; sentences are varied; and vocabulary adds to the persuasiveness of the writing.
- Writing shows clear control of writing conventions, though there may be a few errors.

3 • PROFICIENT

- Writer states opinion and supports it through one or more arguments; uses examples, statistics, anecdotes, or references to experts to persuade.
- Arguments are ordered logically and focus points are clear.
- Writing addresses reader questions and concerns.
- Language is clear; sentence types are varied; vocabulary is specific and persuasive.
- Writing shows control of writing conventions; errors do not interfere with meaning.

2 • NEARLY PROFICIENT

- Writer states opinion but it may be vague or incomplete; examples, statistics, and anecdotes do not sufficiently persuade reader.
- Order of arguments may seem random or choppy; may not focus on one or more arguments.
- Writing does not address reader concerns.
- Language is basic; sentence types are mostly simple; vocabulary is general.
- Errors may interfere with meaning.

1 • DEVELOPING

- Position may be brief or difficult to identify; support is brief.
- Organization of ideas is not clear.
- Reader awareness is not apparent.
- Language is general and vague; sentences may be incomplete or run-on.
- Errors may interfere with meaning.

A School Improvement

Things could always be better, right? Here's your chance to think about something that would be an important improvement at your school. Think about what would make a difference for students, teachers, or both.

GETTING STARTED

To begin, think about what you like about your school. Then think of some complaints you have about your school. Since the purpose of school is to teach students to think and to impart skills and knowledge that will prepare them for life after high school or college, your complaints should connect to learning. Are there factors that get in the way of learning? Does the schedule limit classes students can take? Are classes too big to be effective? Are teachers too busy to help students? Make a list of some problems at your school. Share your list with a classmate, and see if your complaints are similar or different.

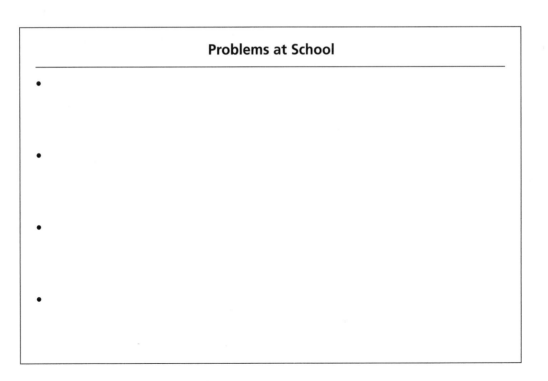

Problems at School

-
-
-
-

READING

Now read the article "Learning to Learn," which is from an online journal called *Technological Horizons in Education*. The author, president of a software company, describes what she considers to be a serious problem in education and recommends a solution. In your writing, you'll also identify a problem and recommend some solutions, so look for the following as you read and code the article with these numbers:

1 = The writer's description of the problem

2 = The solutions she proposes

3 = Persuasive arguments attempting to convince the reader that her solutions will work

Learning to Learn: The Best Strategy for Overall Student Achievement
By Mona Westhaver, president and co-founder, Inspiration Software

Education is at both a crisis and a crossroads. Government rules for higher test scores, diminished state and local funding, and declining student academic success have converged to create an education crisis in the United States.

State and local funding for schools is decreasing. Budget projections are dismal, with more than 30 states expecting more education cutbacks. These cutbacks will result in larger classes and fewer teachers. According to a recent National Assessment of Educational Progress (NAEP), 82% of our nation's 12th-graders performed below the proficient level on the science test. It also showed that only a third of our fourth-graders are able to read at a proficient level, with minority students lagging even further behind. Decreasing resources and increasing needs have created a true education crisis.

There are many proposed solutions for this crisis. The challenge is to focus resources on the most effective strategies; to choose what will really make a difference. Learning to learn—helping students develop thinking skills, learning skills and, most importantly, a passion for learning—is the solution that will have the most long-term and widespread impact. To implement this strategy, students need appropriate resources and tools. In addition, teachers must have excellent training and ongoing professional development to ensure that they are equipped with content knowledge, as well as great instruction and communication skills.

The most important skill students can learn is how to think, learn and be engaged in learning. Students must also learn facts, figures and formulas. Schools need to invest in software and learning tools that promote thinking and can be used across the curriculum.

It is also important for students to know about different student learning styles in order to help them determine how they best learn. Students must learn techniques to clarify thinking, learn difficult concepts, assimilate information and communicate what they have learned. Students must have access to organizing and planning tools. These skills and tools teach students to learn. Not only will they help students build the important skills that they need to be successful academically, they will also serve students as they move into the workforce.

We must also support our schools' most valuable resource: classroom teachers. Without qualified, technology proficient, innovative teachers in the classroom, our investment in other educational resources (e.g., computers, productivity software, textbooks, school buildings) has little value. We must allocate resources to ensure that instructional staff members are fully qualified and are knowledgeable and skilled in today's most effective teaching strategies. We need to guarantee that they have sufficient resources and release time for ongoing professional development. In addition, we must assure that their class sizes are manageable, and that they have the time and support to individualize learning for their students.

The current crisis puts us at a crossroads that will determine whether we, as a society, support our education system by using our limited resources to promote academic achievement for all students, as well as prepare students for work and life in the 21st century.

THINKING AND TALKING

Now work with a partner to complete this exercise.

1. Go back to the article and write *P* next to each paragraph that discusses the problem.

2. Write *S* next to each paragraph that discusses the solution.

3. Highlight or underline the one sentence that best describes the problem.

4. Highlight or underline the one sentence that best describes the solution.

5. Which does the writer discuss more: the problem or the solution?

6. The writer believes that the big problem is made up of smaller problems. Write the sentence you highlighted from Exercise 3 and jot down some smaller problems mentioned.

General Statement of Problem: The Big Problem

More Specific Problems: The Smaller Problems

7. Does the writer use evidence to prove that the problem exists? Write *E* next to the evidence where it occurs.

8. The writer believes that a larger solution is possible by tackling smaller solutions. Write the solution statement you highlighted from Exercise 4 and add smaller solutions below it.

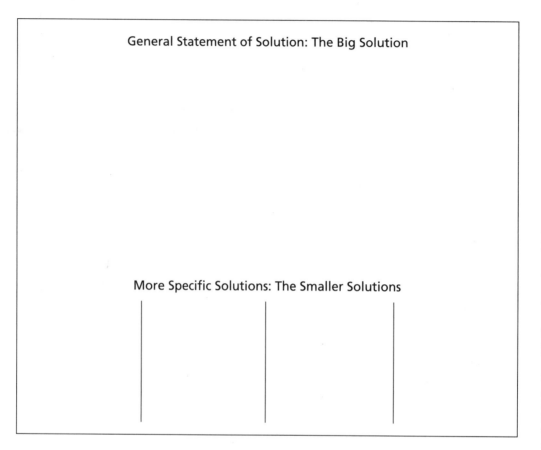

General Statement of Solution: The Big Solution

More Specific Solutions: The Smaller Solutions

9. The writer includes persuasive words and phrases that try to convince the reader of the writer's opinion. Refer to the list below, and then look once more through the article and underline these expressions.

crisis • the most important • must • need

PLANNING

Now go back to your list from the "Getting Started" section and choose a problem at school that you would like to solve. Choose the problem you feel strongest about. Plan your essay by filling in a chart with your ideas as you did in the exercise.

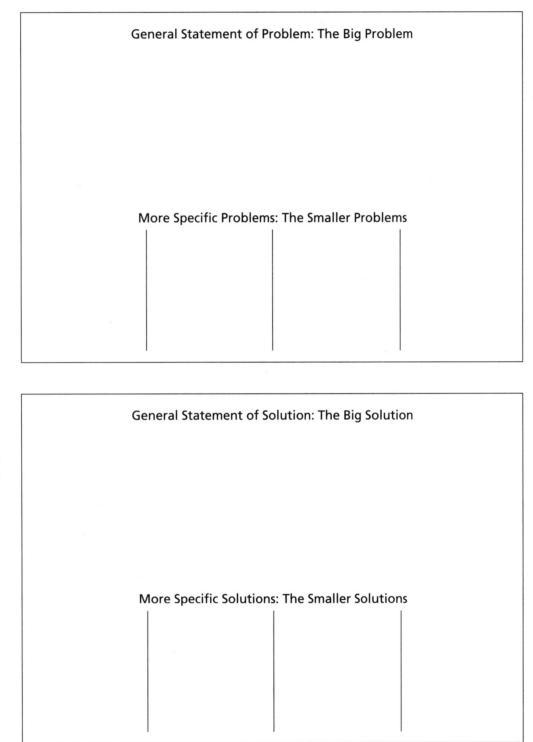

General Statement of Problem: The Big Problem

More Specific Problems: The Smaller Problems

General Statement of Solution: The Big Solution

More Specific Solutions: The Smaller Solutions

REVISING AND EDITING

After writing, review this checklist and make necessary changes.

- ☐ Did you begin by presenting a problem? Did you show evidence of the problem?

- ☐ Did you include specific details (statistics, anecdotes, facts) that show why this problem is serious?

- ☐ Did you propose a solution?

- ☐ Did you include some specific ways to reach this solution?

- ☐ Did you use persuasive language?

- ☐ Did you organize the main ideas of your essay into paragraphs?

- ☐ Check your punctuation. Did you use capital letters, commas, periods, and quotation marks where they belong?

- ☐ How about the ending? Did you remind the reader of the problem and your solution at the end?

- ☐ Did you title your essay?

SELF-ASSESSMENT

Congratulations on completing this process. How would you score this piece of writing?

☐ (4) Commendable ☐ (3) Proficient ☐ (2) Nearly Proficient ☐ (1) Developing

Scoring Guide for Lesson 13:
A School Improvement

GENRE: PROBLEM SOLUTION WRITING

Five Features in Problem Solution Writing
- Description of the Problem
- Presentation of a Solution
- Reader Awareness: Addresses Audience Concerns
- Language: Sentences and Persuasive Vocabulary
- Mechanics: Spelling and Grammar

---

4 • COMMENDABLE
- Describes problem clearly and completely; presents its seriousness or urgency in an original or clever way through convincing use of examples.
- Presents one or more solutions that are creative, practical, and convincing.
- Addresses reader concerns and counterarguments, prioritizes solutions, and shows an ability to be objective.
- Language is lively and expressive; sentence variety and carefully selected vocabulary add to the effectiveness of solutions.
- Writing shows clear control of writing conventions; errors do not cause confusion.

3 • PROFICIENT
- Presents a problem clearly, though the reader may have questions.
- Presents one or more supported solutions.
- Writing attempts to respond to readers' objections through a counterargument.
- Language is clear and sentence types are varied.
- Writing shows control of writing conventions; errors do not interfere with meaning.

2 • NEARLY PROFICIENT
- Presents a problem incompletely.
- Presents one or more solutions that are not developed or convincing.
- Counterargument is not explained or developed.
- Language is basic. Sentence types are mostly simple; vocabulary is general.
- Errors may be distracting.

1 • DEVELOPING
- Presents a vague or incomplete problem.
- Solution is missing or vague or not convincing.
- Writing does not include a convincing counterargument.
- Language is general and vague; sentences may be incomplete or run-on.
- Errors may make it difficult for reader to understand ideas.

Unlikely Thieves

Controversial issues are topics or events in which people have strong (often differing) opinions. We all have strong opinions on some issues. It's usually easy to form a quick opinion, but it's not always easy to defend it. Writing, reading, and talking about an issue can help you think more clearly and express yourself more persuasively. Here's your chance to state your opinion and support it with thoughtful arguments around a current controversial issue.

Most students listen to music, and many have begun to get recordings of their favorite singers or songs from the Internet. Have you done this?

GETTING STARTED

The controversial issue in this chapter has to do with music. So to begin, talk with a classmate and share some of your opinions about music.

Sharing Ideas About Music

1. How often do you listen to music?

2. What's your favorite type of music?

3. Do you buy CDs?

4. Do you listen to the radio? Which station(s)?

5. Do you download music from the Internet?

6. Do you think it's OK to download music from free sites on the Internet even though it's illegal?

READING

Now read this newspaper article about a student's choice to download music from the Internet. As you read, look for facts that support two points of view on this issue.

Recording Industry Has Tough Sell to Beat Free Music

By Jennifer Beauprez, *Denver Post*

Kevin Schiltz is a punk-rock loving, skateboard-toting sophomore at the University of Colorado, and he's part of a powerful force threatening to turn the music industry on its head. Schiltz downloads all of his favorite punk rock and reggae songs off the Internet on file-sharing Web sites. He doesn't care about copyright laws and he doesn't plan to change his behavior—despite a dizzying number of lawsuits expected to be filed by the recording industry. Schiltz says he's heard stories about people being caught, but "CDs cost too much."

Nearly three-quarters of all Internet users Schiltz's age—19 to 29—feel the same way. They don't care that the music they swap online is copyright protected, according to a recent survey. Of Internet users of all ages, 67 percent believe that it's OK to download songs. The survey demonstrates a big problem that many businesses face: people are used to getting things off the Internet for free.

For years, almost no businesses have been able to get people to pay for anything from the Internet. Now big record companies are struggling to stop illegal file swapping. "The recording industry is facing an uphill battle," said one official recently. "People are accustomed to getting things free from the Internet."

Some believe that it is possible to change the habit of getting everything online for free. Flexible pricing and convenience, mixed with a little fear, will be the key to getting people to pay for music online. That includes lawsuits. The music industry effectively shut down Napster several years ago in court, but a number of copycat file-sharing services have since emerged. Now the Recording Industry Association of America is preparing to sue high-volume individual users this month instead.

The tactic might be working. A market research firm reported that the number of songs illegally swapped online dropped to 655 million files from 852 files two months earlier due to the threat of lawsuits. Record companies are also tricking file-sharing sites by uploading what appears to be a popular song but is actually a loop of the song's chorus or a message from the artist.

Legal experts say that the numbers of people breaking copyright laws is a sad statement on the society's lack of respect for moral behavior. They believe that suing individual law-breakers will change the behavior. One business law professor compares illegal file sharing to stealing belongings from someone's home.

Music fans, including Schiltz, say that the limited musical selections presented on radio stations and coming from a few large recording companies do not give listeners access to new and different kinds of music. Clear Channel, the nation's No. 1 radio station owner, for example, owns, programs and sells airtime for 1,225 radio stations. Schiltz repeats, "I think it's hard to find new music."

THINKING AND TALKING

1. Now work with a partner to discuss the *pros* (reasons for) and *cons* (reasons against) of downloading copyrighted music from the Internet without paying anything. Use your own ideas as well as ideas from the newspaper article.

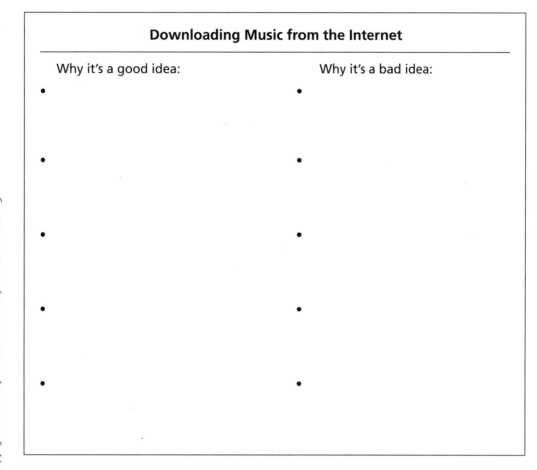

Downloading Music from the Internet

Why it's a good idea:

-
-
-
-
-

Why it's a bad idea:

-
-
-
-
-

2. What do you think musicians would say about downloading their music from the Internet?

_____

_____

_____

3. Should downloading music be legal and should the government support artists and musicians with taxes? Why or why not?

_____

_____

_____

PLANNING

Now clarify your opinion on the issue and organize your ideas. Answer these questions to help you plan your writing.

Unlikely Thieves Planning Guide

1. What is your position on downloading music from the Internet? Do you think it is acceptable or unacceptable?

2. What is one (strong) reason for your opinion? You can use personal experience, facts, or information fro m the newspaper article to develop and support this reason.

3. What is another reason for your opinion? Explain this reason, too.

4. What might someone who disagrees with you think? Address the reader who disagrees with you.

5. Think about a way to support your opinion by making a future prediction.

6. Now pull all your ideas together in a conclusion.

> ### *Writing Prompt: Unlikely Thieves*
>
> Write a persuasive essay in which you present and support your opinion of free downloading of music from the Internet, whether that opinion is pro or con. Use evidence from your reading and examples from your experience to make your writing convincing.

REVISING AND EDITING

After writing, review this checklist and make necessary changes.

- ☐ Did you begin by describing the issue and presenting your opinion?
- ☐ Did you give more than one argument to support your opinion?
- ☐ Did you include specific details (statistics, anecdotes, facts) that show why this issue is serious?
- ☐ Did you include a counterargument?
- ☐ Did you use persuasive language?
- ☐ Did you organize the main ideas of your essay into paragraphs?
- ☐ Check your punctuation. Did you use capital letters, commas, periods, and quotation marks where they belong?
- ☐ How about the ending? Did you remind the reader of the issue and restate your opinion at the end?
- ☐ Did you title your essay?

SELF-ASSESSMENT

Congratulations on completing this process. How would you score this piece of writing?

☐ (4) Commendable ☐ (3) Proficient ☐ (2) Nearly Proficient ☐ (1) Developing

Scoring Guide for Lesson 14: Unlikely Thieves

GENRE: PERSUASIVE WRITING

> ### *Five Features in Persuasive Writing*
> - Clarity of Position and Support of Argument
> - Organization of Ideas and Focus
> - Audience Awareness: Addresses Reader Questions and Concerns
> - Language: Sentences and Persuasive Vocabulary
> - Mechanics: Spelling and Grammar

4 • COMMENDABLE

- Writer's opinion is clearly stated; arguments are well supported through effective use of examples, statistics, anecdotes, or references to experts.
- Arguments are arranged and presented in an order that strengthens the persuasive power of the writing; focus points are clear and logic is easy to follow.
- Writing addresses reader concerns by presenting strong arguments and convincing reasons; may present ideas in a surprising, unusual, or entertaining way.
- Language is precise and lively; sentences are varied; and vocabulary adds to the persuasiveness of the writing.
- Writing shows clear control of writing conventions, though there may be a few errors.

3 • PROFICIENT

- Writer states opinion and supports it through one or more arguments; uses examples, statistics, anecdotes, or references to experts to persuade.
- Arguments are ordered logically and focus points are clear.
- Writing addresses reader questions and concerns.
- Language is clear; sentence types are varied; vocabulary is specific and persuasive.
- Writing shows control of writing conventions; errors do not interfere with meaning.

2 • NEARLY PROFICIENT

- Writer states opinion but it may be vague or incomplete; examples, statistics, and anecdotes do not sufficiently persuade reader.
- Order of arguments may seem random or choppy; may not focus on one or more arguments.
- Writing does not address reader concerns.
- Language is basic; sentence types are mostly simple; vocabulary is general.
- Errors may interfere with meaning.

1 • DEVELOPING

- Position may be brief or difficult to identify; support is brief.
- Organization of ideas is not clear.
- Reader awareness is not apparent.
- Language is general and vague; sentences may be incomplete or run-on.
- Errors may interfere with meaning.

Time to Go Alternative?

This writing lesson gives you a chance to improve your skills at persuasive writing. You will want to collect some facts, formulate or expand an opinion, develop some arguments, then try to persuade your reader to agree with you. You will explain why an alternative fuel vehicle is or isn't a good choice for Americans. Use what you already know and the information you learn and discuss in this lesson to strengthen your writing.

GETTING STARTED

To begin, consider what you know about alternative fuel vehicles (AFVs). Why are they called *alternative*? What do they look like? How do they run? Talk to a classmate and make a list of what you already know about AFVs.

Alternative Fuel Vehicles: What We Know

-
-
-
-
-

READING

Read "New Car Technologies Enter the Mainstream." As you read, highlight or underline and label:

F = Facts about alternative fuel vehicles

Y = Reasons people buy alternative fuel vehicles

N = Reasons people don't buy alternative fuel vehicles

New Car Technologies Enter the Mainstream

By Chuck Squatriglia, *San Francisco Chronicle*

The auto industry, which has shown a single-minded devotion to the internal combustion engine for more than a century, is now developing cars with little more impact on the environment than a bicycle. Alternative fuels have come far in recent years. Ideas considered outlandish just a few years ago are appearing in vehicles on the road now, though in small numbers.

Although gasoline will remain the fuel of choice for the foreseeable future, the world's leading automakers are investing billions of dollars in eco-friendly vehicles. Many industry watchers agree that "sustainable mobility" has become popular because laws are stronger in reducing emissions and technological advances have made alternative fuel vehicles viable.

Hybrid cars, which combine a gasoline engine with a small electric motor, are the latest trend. Toyota and Honda already have "hybrids," with Daimler-Chrysler, Ford, General Motors and Nissan developing new models. We will soon see hybrid sedans, pickups, SUVs and sports cars.

"We're seeing hybrids leave the specialized market and move into the mass market," says Ron Cogan, editor and publisher of *Green Car Journal*. "The novelty of alternative fuel vehicles is wearing off."

None of the advancements in alternative fuel vehicles will mean a thing if consumers don't buy the cars. A recent survey by J. D. Power and Associates found that only 37 percent of consumers said that fuel efficiency influenced their decision when buying a car.

Alternative fuel vehicles have the reputation of being small and underpowered. That makes them a tough sell to consumers who think bigger is better and too much power is just enough. Most consumers aren't willing to pay the higher prices for advanced technology in hybrid vehicles. A base model Honda Civic sedan, for example, starts at $13,010 while the Hybrid version sells for $19,650.

The government is trying to encourage people to "go green" by offering a $2,000 federal tax break to consumers who buy hybrid cars. Alternative fuel vehicles have entered the mainstream. Time will tell if they become the mainstay.

THINKING AND TALKING

After reading, work with a partner to choose the correct answers based on information from the article.

1. The internal combustion engine is
   a. old
   b. new
   c. not yet invented

2. What does eco-friendly mean?
   a. a major impact on the environment
   b. a small impact on the environment
   c. not fuel efficient

3. A hybrid car runs on
   a. only a gasoline engine
   b. only an electric motor
   c. a combined gasoline engine and electric motor

4. According to a recent survey, do most car buyers consider fuel efficiency an important factor?
   a. yes
   b. no

5. Why don't more people buy alternative fuel vehicles?
   a. they're more expensive than traditional cars
   b. they have a reputation for being small and powerless
   c. both of these

6. Does the government want people to buy alternative fuel vehicles?
   a. yes
   b. no

7. Do you know anyone who owns an alternative fuel vehicle? What does this person say about the car's:

Fuel efficiency _____

_____

Ease of driving _____

_____

Appearance _____

_____

Comfort _____

_____

8. What is your opinion of alternative fuel vehicles? Should you or your family some day buy one? Why or why not?

_____

_____

_____

PLANNING

Plan your persuasive essay by taking notes in the chart below.

Time to Go Alternative Planning Chart

Your opinion on alternative fuel vehicles: Should you or your family eventually buy one?

Reason #1 to support your opinion:

Reason #2 to support your opinion:

Reason #3 to support your opinion:

Counterargument—What you say to someone who doesn't agree with you:

Writing Prompt: Time to Go Alternative?

Write an essay stating and supporting your opinion of whether it's time for Americans to "go alternative" in transportation. Do you recommend purchasing an alternative fuel vehicle? You will want to persuade your reader to accept your opinion as to why it is or isn't a good time for Americans to go alternative. Include facts, examples, and personal experiences in your writing. Organize your arguments so that the reader can follow your thinking.

REVISING AND EDITING

After writing, review this checklist and make necessary changes.

- ☐ Did you begin in an interesting or unusual way?
- ☐ Did you make your opinion clear in the first or second paragraph?
- ☐ Did you provide numerous reasons to support your opinion?
- ☐ Did you include specific details (statistics, anecdotes, facts) to convince the reader of your opinion?
- ☐ Did you include a counterargument?
- ☐ Did you use persuasive language?
- ☐ Did you organize the main ideas of your essay into paragraphs?
- ☐ Check your punctuation. Did you use capital letters, commas, periods, and quotation marks where they belong?
- ☐ How about the ending? Did you restate your opinion in an emphatic way?
- ☐ Did you title your essay?

SELF-ASSESSMENT

Congratulations on completing this process. How would you score this piece of writing?

☐ (4) Commendable   ☐ (3) Proficient   ☐ (2) Nearly Proficient   ☐ (1) Developing

Scoring Guide for Lesson 15:
Time to Go Alternative?

GENRE: PERSUASIVE WRITING

Five Features in Persuasive Writing

- Clarity of Position and Support of Argument
- Organization of Ideas and Focus
- Audience Awareness: Addresses Reader Questions and Concerns
- Language: Sentences and Persuasive Vocabulary
- Mechanics: Spelling and Grammar

---

4 • COMMENDABLE

- Writer's opinion is clearly stated; arguments are well supported through effective use of examples, statistics, anecdotes, or references to experts.
- Arguments are arranged and presented in an order that strengthens the persuasive power of the writing; focus points are clear; and logic is easy to follow.
- Writing addresses reader concerns by presenting strong arguments and convincing reasons; may present ideas in a surprising, unusual, or entertaining way.
- Language is precise and lively; sentences are varied; and vocabulary adds to the persuasiveness of the writing.
- Writing shows clear control of writing conventions, though there may be a few errors.

3 • PROFICIENT

- Writer states opinion and supports it through one or more arguments; uses examples, statistics, anecdotes, or references to experts to persuade.
- Arguments are ordered logically and focus points are clear.
- Writing addresses reader questions and concerns.
- Language is clear; sentence types are varied; vocabulary is specific and persuasive.
- Writing shows control of writing conventions; errors do not interfere with meaning.

2 • NEARLY PROFICIENT

- Writer states opinion but it may be vague or incomplete; examples, statistics, and anecdotes do not sufficiently persuade reader.
- Order of arguments may seem random or choppy; may not focus on one or more arguments.
- Writing does not address reader concerns.
- Language is basic; sentence types are mostly simple; vocabulary is general.
- Errors may interfere with meaning.

1 • DEVELOPING

- Position may be brief or difficult to identify; support is brief.
- Organization of ideas is not clear.
- Reader awareness is not apparent.
- Language is general and vague; sentences may be incomplete or run-on.
- Errors may interfere with meaning.

Copyright © 2005 by Meredith Pike-Baky and Gerald Fleming

Student Exemplars

We have included nine student exemplars to assist you in using the rubrics to evaluate your students' writing. Each of these exemplars is a *first draft effort* responding to prompts in this book. (Refer to Chapter Five for two additional samples to review the scoring procedure.)

For each of these student examples, we have added some brief comment explaining the score and sometimes making recommendations for improvement. The samples represent writing from several genres and reflect how a range of students (boys, girls, native speakers, nonnative speakers, middle school, high school) responded to the prompts within the hour time limit. Use the exemplars to help you translate the rubrics for instruction or revision. Add to these examples with your own students' (anonymous) papers.

Exemplars Demonstrating COMMENDABLE ACHIEVEMENT

Title	Genre	Lesson	Score Point
The Cormorant's Tale	Response to Poetry	9. Responding to "The Cormorant's Tale"	4
Jamba Juice Smoothies	Information	10. Here's Something Cool!	4

Exemplars Demonstrating PROFICIENT ACHIEVEMENT

Title	Genre	Lesson	Score Point
When I Was a Small Child	Personal Narration	2. A Childhood Passion	3
Are Potato Chips Replacing an Apple in the Future?	Persuasion	11. Junk Food Lunches?	3
No Title	Information	10. Here's Something Cool!	3

Exemplars Demonstrating NEARLY PROFICIENT ACHIEVEMENT

Title	Genre	Lesson	Score Point
My Special Place	Personal Description	1. A Personal Oasis	2
Don't Judge Something You Don't Know	Response to Literature	8. Responding to "Boar Out There"	2
No Title	Persuasion	12. Key to Success	2

Exemplar Demonstrating DEVELOPING ACHIEVEMENT

Title	Genre	Lesson	Score Point
Dear Mr. A,	Problem Solution	13. A School Improvement	1

SCORE POINT 4: COMMENDABLE ACHIEVEMENT

Genre: Response to Poem   Lesson 9: Responding to "The Cormorant's Tale"

"The Cormorant's Tale"

This poem, "The Cormorant's Tale" can relate to many people's lives. Some people feel exactly like the cormorant. They might feel tortured, trapped, used, or upset because someone isn't treating them with the respect they deserve. You might feel this way if you have enemies or even with your families.

I'm one of the people who isn't treated fairly. Some people aren't exactly my friends so they think it's cool just to talk about me behind my back. I felt exactly the way the cormorant feels. I had felt like there was a giant ring around my neck that they controlled. It felt like they had power that I could not obtain. I eventually broke that ring. I broke it by realizing that they really didn't have that much power over me, that it was all in my head. The ring broke off easily.

The poem used a very strong metaphor. They put human emotions into the cormorant so that they can see the way that the cormorant is feeling. Paul Fleischman showed the problem through the cormorant's point of view.

At the end of the poem, the cormorant says:

"I want to be free and unfettered. As free as a fish."

I think this means that being a bird, the cormorant is trapped inside the ring. He would much rather swim in the ocean with the other fishes. From the cormorants point of view, fishes have all the freedom they need.

Let's go back to how the poem relates to me. I have been used by other people a lot. Even my friends use me. My friends are like my owner and I'm the cormorant. They hold power over me. Sometimes I help them with some homework and what do I get . . . zip, nada, nil, NOTHING. Another example is sometimes I give them nice presents that take me a long time to earn. When it comes time for them to give me a little something, I get something but it's not a very good something. It shows that they don't really care or they're too lazy.

I am the cormorant. We are both trapped, confused, and exploited. We feel like we're not treated fairly. We both feel tortured and disrespected. The cormorant will be free, and so will I.

Comments:

In this piece, the writer takes an idea (bondage of the cormorant) and applies it to her experience. She shows how Fleischman uses personification and metaphor to argue for the cormorant's right to freedom. Though there are a few language mistakes in this piece, the organization begins and ends with the same ideas and develops a reasonable interpretation in the middle.

SCORE POINT 4: COMMENDABLE ACHIEVEMENT

Genre: Information Writing   Lesson 10: Here's Something Cool!

Jamba Juice Smoothies

Do you know how the tastier a food is, the less healthy it is? Well, would you like to be introduced to a healthy and tasty drink? I'm Bonnie, and I'd like to tell you all about Jamba Juice.

Jamba Juice is a smoothie, made of many fruits. It is a blend of 3 to 4 servings of fruits, with added yogurt and ice. Jamba Juice is blended, squeezed, and made to order, so you can be guaranteed that it'll be fresh! Can anyone drink Jamba Juice, you ask? Yes, Jamba Juice is for anyone, for everyone. The flavors are great, and there is a big variety of flavors. Razzmatazz, Berry Lime Sublime, Citrus Squeeze, Chocolate Moo'd, Peach Pleasure, Mango-a-Go-go, and Banana Berry are only some of the many flavors that fall under Functional Flavors™, Berry Bliss™, Tropical Getaways™, Citrus Sensations™, and Enlightened Smoothies™.

Jamba Juice is very healthy, and it'll keep you cool and refreshed on a hot summer day, but also energized on a chilly winter day. How is Jamba Juice energizing? This is how: there are lots of protein and vitamins in the smoothie, and the optional boosts give extra nutrients. Just to name some of the boosts, there is the Fiber Boost, Vita Boost, Protein Boost, Burner Boost, and Energy Boost. For those of you who don't desire a lot of calories, the Enlightened Smoothies™ are just for you, with one-third less calories!

Now, let me share with you my first experience with Jamba Juice. I bought a 16 ounce Jamba Juice, for only $2.95! How much better could it get? Not much! The flavor I got was Razzmatazz, with blended rasberry, strawberry, sorbet, frozen yogurt, and ice. It was delicious, heavenly! The Razzmatazz was an attractive magenta color, with bits of rasberry seeds in it, and the smoothie was cool and refreshing, just what everybody loves!

Let me ask you something: do you want some Jamba Juice now? You do? Well, let me tell you something else. A 16 oz. is only $2.95, an original is only $3.75, and for $4.25, you get a power sized Jamba Juice smoothie!

Once again, try Jamba Juice, the most energizing, healthy, and tasty, smoothie in the whole world! I guarantee you that you'll enjoy it, and you'll be going back for more! So see you at Jamba Juice!

Comments:

In this piece, the writer consistently supports her claim that Jamba Juice is both tasty and nutritious. She responds to reader questions and enthusiastically and convincingly points out why the variety of drinks, priced reasonably, is something to consider. This is upbeat and competent.

SCORE POINT 3: PROFICIENT ACHIEVEMENT

Genre: Personal Narrative   Lesson 2: A Childhood Passion

When I Was a Small Child

When I was a small child, I imagined that when I grew up I would become an astronaut. I thought it would be cool to set foot on the moon and see the preserved footprints of Neil Armstrong.

I would imagine myself in the cockpit of The Challenger flipping switches and pressing buttons, I was in control of a mechanical behemoth of my imagination.

"Houston we have a problem!"

But I would fix the problem by sticking bubble gum in an oxygen leak, duct taping a hole or simply tying down a snapped chunk of the wing.

I thought that being an explorer of the unexplored would be the job for me. I could be on a different planet, maybe I'd be the first to set foot on Mars. If I were an astronaut I would be a hero.

Though I was young I knew that your body didn't age in space. If I went when I was young I could stay a child forever, I could live in a Neverland, I would be Peter Pan.

In space there is no gravity, so I could bounce around. When you hang upside down your not really hanging upside down.

Now that I'm older, being an astronaut seems a little risky, with two spaceships blowing up and all. Though I don't wan't to be a spaceman, I would still love to look at the pictures that the spacemen themselves took while risking their lives.

All in all now that I'm older it doesn't seem so fun to go to space. I think it's nice where I am and I don't wan't to another town let alone another planet. Anyway Earth is the only place for Humans.

Comments:

This piece is a clear and amusing description of the writer's desire to be an astronaut when younger. Specific memories (Neverland) and details about astronauts (references to the *Challenger*, Neil Armstrong, etc.) reflect the writer's passion. Vocabulary and sentence variety keep the reader engaged. Though there is a clear beginning, middle, and end, the brief paragraphs become a list of memories and make the piece choppy. Developing and elaborating more fully on one of the memories would move this to a 4.

SCORE POINT 3: PROFICIENT ACHIEVEMENT

Genre: Persuasion   Lesson 11: Junk Food Lunches?

Are Potato Chips Replacing an Apple in the Future?

Fourth period just ended and I'm on my way to the cafeteria to buy lunch. I stop by the vending machine and I look at the choices: potato chips, soft drinks, fruit juice, fruit cups, and muffins. "They're hard picks to choose from," I think to myself, "But, mom says that I can buy anything I want for lunch. Potato chips taste so much better than a muffin and a soda would definitely taste sweeter than plain fruit juice." Afterwards, I just buy the potato chips and a soft drink for lunch. When I'm finished, I find that I'm still hungry and I have no more money left to buy anything else. What should I do? I know! I borrow some money from my friends and somehow pay them back.

Though this is something I made up straight off of my head, believe it or not, children happen to come to this situation many times in school life. In case if you didn't understand what the meanings of that paragraph meant, I state them right now.

First, potato chips and sodas are in the unhealthy food group, or as we people say it, the junk food category. By replacing fruits and muffins for lunch, junk food won't give you the nutrients you need for daily life. From this, you could become obese (or overweight), and if fat continues to clog your arteries, you could get a heart attack, which then could lead to death. Right now in America, half or more Americans are obese.

Second, junk food doesn't really do much good to fill you up. Though a bag of chips may seem like it equals to a regular-size muffin, it doesn't fill you up nearly as good as a muffin. Why you ask? Because chips may contain oil and salt, and nutrients are what you need to fill you up. For example, if you have a donut for dinner instead of a bowl of rice or pasta, you'd notice that once you finish your donut, you'd crave for more while once you finish eating a bowl of rice or pasta, you'd feel filled up and satisfied with how you feel, whether it's physically or emotionally.

Third, though it doesn't really seem germane to this topic, junk food wastes your lunch money! What happens when a child runs out of money and need money to buy food to eat because he/she is still hungry? He/she borrow money from other people! But, look at the alternate side of this solution. If he/she runs out of money everyday and continues having loans, then when is she going to owe back what she owes?

If you've seeing this problem the way I'm seeing it, then you should probably be agreeing with me that Congress should do something about the amount of junk food being sold in schools. Though I understand that schools have vending machines that sell junk food so they can make some money for funding school necessities, I think that they should increase the amount of nutritional foods being sold in vending machines and decreasing the amount of junk food. Once again, I'm going to state that I would most definitely like Congress to put standards on junk food.

Comments:

This persuasive piece begins with an engaging anecdote that makes the issue relevant. However, the writer spends lots of time developing arguments against eating junk food and not linking this to school vending machines or cafeteria choices. (The task of this prompt is not to argue the benefits or disadvantages of junk food, but to argue whether junk food should be restricted to students in school.) The writer concludes by briefly returning to the topic, but the essay is mostly a thorough response to a different prompt. The arguments are clear and logically presented and there is control of most conventions.

SCORE POINT 3: PROFICIENT ACHIEVEMENT

Genre: Information Writing   Lesson 10: Here's Something Cool!

No Title

Hello. I am an 11 year old 7th grader. I'd like to talk about a Game system called "Game Boy Advance SP." This product is the greatest gameboy so far. I think you should buy it because it is great and I mean GREAT for kids. This gameboy has some special features that the other gameboys don't have. This game system is small and portable so you can take this anywhere.

I love this gameboy because you can even play videos on it. If you're a kid and love to watch cartoons, this can play episodes of your favorite shows. The name of some episodes are: Pokemon, The fairy odd parents, Spongebob squarepants, Harry Potter, Yu-Gi-Oh, Jimmy Neutron, etc etc. There are a LOT of shows you can watch. Get these videos now because they won't be around for a long time!

This gameboy is the only portable one that you can fit in your pocket. It looks like a regular gameboy but you can fold it in half!!! It even has a small light in the screen so you can play in the dark. Also you don't need batteries. In the package it already gives you a thing to recharge where the batteries are suppose to be. There are a lot of games you can get for the system. Examples of games are: Pokemon, Leaf Green and Fire Red, Super Mario, Warrio land 4, and Oragon ball 2 Budakai 3.

Finally, I think that you should buy this game because it is great, fun and portable. Its cheap really fun to play with and, it's just GREAT!!!!

Comments:

This paper is clear, succinct, and enthusiastic. It is also repetitious. We recommend that the writer extend his ideas by integrating some of the following strategies in a revision: use comparison (rather than repetition) to help the reader appreciate the new Gameboy, explain *why* it's a benefit to have lots of videos, not need batteries, and fold it in half. This paper is a good example of a skeleton that could use some fleshing out to earn a 4.

SCORE POINT 2: NEARLY PROFICIENT ACHIEVEMENT

Genre: Descriptive Writing   Lesson 1: A Personal Oasis

My Special Place

I am a quiet person and I like to read, play imaginary games or just sit and think about different things. To do all this I have found a special place in my house, the living room. It's bright with sun light on sunny days making the room warm and friendly. Decorated in a creamy white and an earthy peace gives the right nice touch to it.

After a tiring day at school, if my afternoon is free, I usally come home, make my self a snack and setle down on the soft, sun warmed couch pillows with a book. Peaceful and quiet in the living room I'll read for hours or pretend I'm a princess with a hundred maids in waiting or think about different things, any thing. Or else I'll just lie in the warm sun resting and maybe fall asleep. What ever it is I love to be in living room. I feel as if it's the central place of the house for me, as my own bedroom is darker in color and atmosphere.

The living room, my special place holds lots of treasures and I never want to lose them.

Comments:

This paper is clear, but it is undeveloped. The beginning is promising as the writer reveals information about herself that leads to the special place, but so many questions about her special place remain unanswered. What's in the room? What colors or objects help the reader imagine this place? Developing the comparison to the writer's bedroom would also help the reader imagine the living room.

SCORE POINT 2: NEARLY PROFICIENT ACHIEVEMENT

Genre: Response to Literature   Lesson 8: Responding to "Boar Out There"

Don't Judge Something You Don't Know

In my opinion, one of the important idea communicated in the story was when Jenny came face to face with the boar and learned that it was more scare of her than she was of it.

During this scene from the story, the girl not only saw how the boar looked like but also the fear in him. Jenny stood there in front of the boar both staring at each other. She saw that it didn't look like how she imagin, and it was bleeding. There was silence between the two, nothing was there to be heard but the wind and the leaves. From this moment she knew the boar was scare of bluejays and little girls, (people).

I think in this scene the author showed that the boar was not as dangerous and scary as any of the townspeople thought. The author tried to show that there really was nothing to be afraid of, the boar was more scare than probably any of those people. The townspeople never really met the boar before yet they fear him. In other words, they were afraid of something that they hardly knew anything about. None of them have really encouter with the boar like what Jenny did. To me, that was quite pathetic. The boar was injuried and much more poor than any of the people yet it was feared by them like it was a dragon.

I also think the author was trying to use this scene to show us something outside of the story. The author probably tried to show that you shouldn't be scare to come in contact with something or someone you don't know about or know little about. Like in the story, the townspeople judged the boar to be dangerous and scary, but was the boar really like that. No, it wasn't. So you shouldn't judge something or someone by anything unless there is prove. If the townspeople had encounter the boar like Jenny, they'll know the boar is just another helpless animal whos alone and afraid.

So basicly from this scene the author kid of shows the main point and the moral of the story. But this is only what I think. Again, the moral is don't judge something when you really don't know if that's true.

Comments:

The writer of this paper, a second language learner, has made a noble stab at literary analysis. After an abrupt introduction (without citing the story title), she summarizes the scene and goes on to analyze what it means in the story and how it applies to everyone. The ideas are clear and supported; the language errors, however, are distracting and keep this paper from getting a higher score. With an opportunity to rewrite the introduction and correct some word endings, this paper could easily be a 3.

SCORE POINT 2: NEARLY PROFICIENT ACHIEVEMENT

Genre: Persuasion   Lesson 12: Key to Success

No Title

I think the key to success is to be a hard-working student. By being a hard worker you will learn more information and knowledge. You'll do well on tests, go to a good college and get a good job.

Being a hard-working student is one of the best ways to live a balanced life. When you work hard in school, it is easier to work hard at home and help your family. I have the experience of having been a hard-working student since fifth grade. This is because my fifth grade teacher gave me far more homework than any other teacher. At that time, I almost fell into my lazy zone because I got tired of doing homework until 10pm every night. But I did the work she assigned and I got a higher grade. I respected her for pushing me.

Once I learned how to be a hard-working student, my grades improved. Being a hard-worker will bring you success in life.

Comments:

While this paper is organized and the writer has used personal experience to support the main idea, the writing is too brief to be persuasive. The writer can describe what he means by working hard. He can give specific examples of people who achieved success through hard work, elaborate more on his experience in fifth grade, and explain more deeply the link between school and work. Any of these additions will improve this paper.

SCORE POINT 1: DEVELOPING ACHIEVEMENT

Genre: Problem Solution   Lesson 13: A School Improvement

Dear Mr. A,

I understand that you are looking for a solution about the school garbage problem.

The garbage problem is capable of starting a rodent infestation and it has already attracted bugs. Another thing is that birds come in to the yard and eat the remaining scraps of our lunch. Dogs and cats would be another problem.

So I suggest that there should be punishment to solved this problem. One way is to pay a money fine. Another way is to give a lunchtime detention. While serving detention, you must pick up trash.

I hope these suggestions are able to help solve our problem.

Sincerely,

Hopeful

Comments:

This response to the problem of school garbage is incomplete. References to rodents, bugs, birds, dogs, and cats are confusing. The writer can improve this piece by describing the problem more fully (Where is the garbage? How does it get there? How long has it been a problem?) and explaining the proposed solution. The solution is sketchy.

Narrative Writing Strategies

Use this list to learn and practice many ways to develop your narrative writing. Choose only some of them (5–6 is a good guideline) when you're writing a narrative essay.

☐ *Names* of people, places, and events can make your narrative more vivid.

☐ *Visual details* are the specific colors, shapes, textures, or actions you noticed when the event occurred. They help the reader see what you saw.

☐ *Sounds* are what you remember hearing during the event.

☐ *Tastes* are flavors you imagine or remember.

☐ *Smells* are the odors or fragrances you associate with real or imagined experiences.

☐ *Feelings* describe your fears, expectations, worries, hopes, or happiness at the time of an event—or now, as you remember it.

☐ *Measurements* are specific details about size, shape, date, and time.

☐ *Dialogue* is what people said. Dialogue can advance the action and help the reader get to know the characters.

☐ *Interior monologue* is what you thought but didn't say out loud. Interior monologue is what you said silently to yourself and is underlined—or italicized, if you use a computer. (In a book, it would also usually be in italic type, the way it is in Lesson 4.)

☐ *Humor* makes the reader laugh and helps describe how the writer felt about a real or imagined experience.

☐ *Suspense* is saving the ending as a surprise for the reader.

☐ *Comparison* helps the reader understand how the people, places, actions, or feelings are similar to or different from something else more familiar. Writers can use similes and metaphors in addition to statements of comparison to show how things are similar or different.

☐ *Pacing* is how quickly or slowly you tell the story to hold your reader's interest.

☐ A *title* for your narrative can draw the reader in and highlight the important ideas.

☐ *Reflection* tells the reader what you've learned or how you feel about the event now.

☐ *Talking* directly to the reader can make your writing more personal and tell the reader how you feel.

Persuasive Writing Pitfalls

In persuasive essays, you want to develop your ideas logically to convince your reader to agree with you. If your writing is illogical or irrational, it won't be persuasive. Students sometimes make these four logic errors when writing persuasive essays. You should try to avoid these.

1. JUMPING TO CONCLUSIONS

It's very easy to make hasty generalizations, but they often fall apart if you look at them carefully.

Examples:

All homework is boring.

Girls can learn to play sports better from boys.

Tip:

Avoid words like *everybody, all,* and *never.* Be specific. Qualify broad statements by using phrases like *can be, are sometimes,* or *some people find:*

- Sometimes homework is boring, especially when I'm not interested in the subject we're studying.

- It can be helpful for girls to learn to play sports from boys because some boys play sports a lot and have become really good at them.

2. STEREOTYPING

A stereotype is a special kind of hasty generalization applied to people. Nobody is simple enough to match a stereotype.

Examples:

Kids who speak Spanish are shy.

Happy families make happy children.

Tip:

Use evidence to support your statements:

- Some Spanish-speaking students are hesitant to speak Spanish at school. Although Keren and Denise speak perfect Spanish, they only speak English in the classroom.
- Children who come from happy families are more likely to be happy themselves. When there is a lot of yelling and frustration in a home, kids are more likely to act that way with others.

3. USING RED HERRINGS

A red herring is a statement that has no direct relevance to the topic. Writers sometimes use red herrings on purpose, so people don't think about the real issue, but readers who notice red herrings usually decide to ignore everything the writer has to say.

Example:

When put in large groups, boys get in trouble. For instance, I was at my friend's house for a sleepover and we decided to put shaving cream on his sister's face.

Tip:

Reread the prompt after you have planned your writing. Always read over your writing and take time to cut out sentences that are off topic:

- When put in large groups, boys sometimes get in trouble. For example, when I go to the movies with a group of friends, I'm more likely to make a lot of noise than when I am with just one friend.

4. OVERSIMPLIFICATION

Oversimplification denies the complexity of an idea, so you can't get to the real truth.

Example:

Mandatory summer school makes students frustrated and causes them to lose interest in studying.

Tip:

Even if you're sure that one thing is the cause of another, it may not be the *only* cause.

- Mandatory summer school can make students frustrated and cause them to lose interest in studying. It's helpful to have a break from school in the summer so you're fresh and interested again when you go back.

Writing Sample Form

Please enlarge when photocopying to accommodate students' writing.

Writing Sample

Do not write in this box.

START ESSAY HERE

Please print

Last Name _____ First Name _____

Teacher _____ Grade _____ Period _____

School _____ Date _____

Average Score

_____

_____

_____

_____

_____

_____

_____

_____

_____

_____

_____

_____

_____

_____

_____

_____

_____

_____

_____

_____

_____

_____

_____

_____

_____

_____

Batch Sheet Form

BATCH SHEET

Assessment (Genre/Topic/Date) _____ Batch #_____

Student ID #	Final Score	Reader #3	Reader #2	Reader #1
1.				
2.				
3.				
4.				
5.				
6.				
7.				
8.				
9.				
10.				
11.				
12.				
13.				
14.				
15.				
Reader Initials →				

(When you've completed scoring a batch, fold your column under to obscure scores for the next reader.)

Bibliography

Cooper, C. R., and Odell, L. (eds.). *Evaluating Writing: The Role of Teachers' Knowledge About Text, Learning, and Culture.* Urbana, Ill.: National Council of Teachers of English, 1999.

Education Week, July 11, 2001.

Hillocks, G., Jr. *Teaching Writing as Reflective Practice.* New York: Teachers College Press, 1995.

Hillocks, G., Jr. *The Testing Trap: How State Writing Assessments Control Learning.* New York: Teachers College Press, 2002.

Lewin, L. *Paving the Way in Reading and Writing: Strategies and Activities to Support Struggling Students in Grades 6–12.* San Francisco: Jossey-Bass, 2003.

Smith, M., and Wilhelm, J. *Reading Don't Fix No Chevys.* Portsmouth, N.H.: Heinemann, 1998.

Spardel, V., and Stiggins, R. *Creating Writers: Linking Assessment and Instruction.* New York: Longman, 1997.

INDEX

"Education is the Key to Latino Success," by Mauricio Torres-Benavides:

"Education is the Key to Latino Success" by Mauricio Torres-Benavides, *Marin Independent Journal,* 3/26/03. Reprinted with permission from Matt Wilson, Executive Editor, Marin Independent Journal and Mauricio Torres-Benavides.

"Learning to Learn," Mona Westhaver:

"Learning to Learn: The Best Strategy for Overall Student Achievement" by Mona Westhaver from *T.H.E. Journal Online,* June 2003. Adapted with permission of T.H.E. Journal via the Copyright Clearance Center, and the author.

"Recording Industry Has Tough Sell to Beat Free Music," Jennifer Beauprez:

"Recording Industry Has Tough Sell to Beat Free Music" by Jennifer Beauprez from the *Denver Post,* reprinted in the *Marin Independent Journal,* September 8, 2003. Reprinted with permission of the *Denver Post.*

"New Car Technologies Enter the Mainstream," Chuck Squatriglia:

"New Car Technologies Enter the Mainstream" by Chuck Squatriglia from the *San Francisco Chronicle,* September 25, 2003. Copyright © 2003 by *San Francisco Chronicle.* Adapted with permission of *San Francisco Chronicle* via Copyright Clearance Center.